FAITH METAPHORS
50 INTERACTIVE OBJECT LESSONS FOR YOUTH MINISTRY

Loveland, Colorado

Group's R.E.A.L. Guarantee to you:

Every Group resource incorporates our R.E.A.L. approach to ministry—
a unique philosophy that results in long-term retention and life
transformation. It's ministry that's:

This is EARL. He's R.E.A.L. mixed up. (Get it?)

Relational
Because student-to-student interaction enhances learning and builds Christian friendships.

Experiential
Because what students experience sticks with them up to 9 times longer than what they simply hear or read.

Applicable
Because the aim of Christian education is to be both hearers and doers of the Word.

Learner-based
Because students learn more and retain it longer when the process is designed according to how they learn best.

Faith Metaphors
Copyright © 2002 Group Publishing, Inc.

Visit our Web site: **www.grouppublishing.com**

Credits

Contributing Authors: Tim Baker, Debbie Gowensmith, Stacy Haverstock, Mikal Keefer, Jan Kershner, Jim Kochenburger, Pamela Malloy, Julie Meiklejohn, Mark A. Rempel, Siv M. Ricketts, Christina Schofield, Kelli B. Trujillo, and Helen Turnbull
Editor: Julie Meiklejohn
Creative Development Editor: Amy Simpson
Chief Creative Officer: Joani Schultz
Copy Editor: Janis Sampson
Art Director: Randy Kady
Cover Art Director: Jeff A. Storm
Cover Designer: Alan Furst Inc.
Cover Photographer: Daniel Treat
Computer Graphic Artist: Stephen Beer
Illustrator: Steve Duffendack
Production Manager: Dodie Tipton

Unless otherwise noted, Scripture taken from the HOLY BIBLE, NEW INTERNATIONAL VERSION®. Copyright © 1973, 1978, 1984 by International Bible Society. Used by permission of Zondervan Publishing House. All rights reserved.

Library of Congress Cataloging-in-Publication Data
Faith metaphors : 50 interactive object lessons for youth ministry.
    p. cm.
  Includes indexes.
  ISBN 0-7644-2301-0 (alk. paper)
  1. Church work with youth. 2. Youth--Religious life. I. Group Publishing.
  BV4447 .F34 2001
  259'.23--dc21
                          2001054313

Printed in the United States of America.
10 9 8 7 6 5 4 3 2   11 10 09 08 07 06 05 04 03 02

Contents

Introduction

Question: What do these three scenes have in common?

- One teenager hides in a darkened room, gripping a laser pointer tightly. Several other teenagers carefully search for him or her with their flashlights.
- A group of teenagers works together to lift a heavy barbell.
- One teenager uses a remote control to "control" his or her friends.

Answer: All of the teenagers in these scenes are being impacted with important truths about God, Jesus, and the Bible—through the use of object lessons!

The object lessons found in *Faith Metaphors* will help teenagers understand how it feels, smells, sounds, tastes, and looks to be a Christian by providing concrete, real-world connections to more abstract concepts. Each object lesson centers around one specific, easy-to-obtain object. Teenagers are encouraged to interact with the object and each other in creative, fun ways to bring them to "aha" moments in which they see true glimpses of God's power and glory in the mundane.

These lessons use objects such as credit card applications, a box of cereal, and even gerbils to help your teenagers understand more about God and his plans for their lives. Many of the object lessons include "FYI" boxes to provide helpful information as you plan and carry out these lessons.

In addition, each object lesson ends with a "Taking It Further" option, which provides valuable ideas and resources to turn the object lesson into a full-fledged lesson or lesson series.

The lessons are arranged in alphabetical order according to topic to make it easy for you to choose an experience for your teenagers. In addition, *Faith Metaphors* ends with a Scripture index to help you further.

So go ahead—choose an everyday object, and use *Faith Metaphors* to create an out-of-this-world experience your teenagers won't ever forget!

Approved!

The Topic: Acceptance

The Point: Students will learn to accept and reach out to people who are sometimes overlooked, just as God reaches out to each of us.

The Scripture: Acts 9:10-19

The Object: Credit card applications

The Supplies: You'll need a Bible, blank credit card applications, pens, and white paper correction fluid (optional).

The Object Lesson

If necessary, white out any personal information on the credit card applications. You'll need one for each student in your class (you may need to make photocopies).

For a fun way to distribute the forms, you might want to place them inside envelopes and put them in an actual mailbox in your classroom. Throw in other pieces of junk mail to add to the effect.

Give each student a blank credit card application and a pen. Ask students to fill in the forms with fictitious information, including an imaginary salary figure and occupation. When students have completed the applications, collect them and say: **Before issuing credit cards, companies determine whether it is risky to loan money to people based on the personal information they have provided. People are given credit or denied credit based on whether the company thinks they are reliable and capable of paying back what they owe. In some cases, people may be overlooked and denied credit simply because they have never borrowed money before or because their ages or circumstances make them potential risks. Let's sort through these applications you have filled out and decide who to accept and deny based on these guidelines.**

The movie *Remember the Titans* is built on the theme of acceptance of those who are "different." Consider opening your class with previewed clips from this film to start teenagers thinking about what it means to be accepted.

FYI

Before you go through the applications, you may want to work together with your students to determine standards for acceptance such as minimum salary and minimum age.

Discuss each form with your students and decide which applicants should be accepted and given credit.

After you've gone through all of the applications, say: **Thankfully, God doesn't accept or reject us based on whether we deserve his favor or can ever pay him back. Even though we have nothing to offer God, he accepts us because of his grace and love for us, not because of our worth.**

Have a volunteer read Acts 9:10-19 aloud, and say: **Saul would definitely have been considered "high risk." But God saw the good in him and asked Ananias to do the same. Even though Saul had made some serious mistakes, God was willing to accept him and make him really important.**

Ask: • **How might history have been different if Ananias had refused to help Saul?**

• **How does it feel to be excluded?**

• **How does God's unconditional acceptance of you change how you view others?**

• **What can you do to include "forgotten" and overlooked people in your circle of friends?**

Close with a prayer, thanking God for the way he accepts us as his children.

Taking It Further

Share with your teenagers a story about the Wemmicks from the children's book *Tell Me the Secrets* by Max Lucado. This story is about a wooden man who finds out he is valuable despite what his peers think because his maker loves and accepts him as he is. Challenge teenagers to identify the "stars" and "dots" in their own lives and strive to seek their Maker's acceptance more than the acceptance of their peers.

Laser Tag!

The Topic: The Bible

The Point: Students will learn that the Bible points us to God, shows us the seriousness of sin, and has the power to transform lives.

The Scripture: Psalm 119:1-18; Romans 1:16

The Object: A red-light laser pointer

The Supplies: You'll need Bibles, a red-light laser pointer, flashlights, and black trash bags and tape (optional).

The Object Lesson

Prepare an open space for a game of laser tag. Cover any windows with black trash bags, and move chairs and other objects to the sides of the area. Be sure there are plenty of potential hiding places around the area.

Give each person a flashlight, and tell students they're going to play a fun game of laser tag. Hold up the red-light laser pointer, and explain the rules of the game by saying: **One person will hide with this laser pointer, and everyone else will attempt to find him or her. In order to "expose" the person who is hiding, you must be close enough to shine your flashlight on him or her without first being "tagged" by the laser. If you get tagged by the laser, you're out for the rest of the game.**

Explain that the hiding person should wait a few minutes after everyone has entered the room before he or she begins tagging people, and ask the hider not to shine the light directly into anyone's eyes. Give one person the laser pointer, and ask him or her to hide in the playing area. As the rest of the students enter the playing area, encourage them to remain as invisible as possible, using their flashlights only when absolutely necessary. Continue to play until everyone has been tagged or until the hider has been caught.

> **FYI**
>
> This would be a good late-night outdoor activity at a retreat or a camp!

Collect the flashlights and the laser pointer and say: **This laser is used to point at things. It can penetrate darkness for**

more than one hundred feet. Lasers can heal or destroy and are used in different types of surgery.

Similarly, the Bible is a really powerful tool and capable of healing people. It exposes sin, showing how dark a world apart from God would be. The Bible points us to God—it shows us what God is like, what he expects from us, and his plan for our lives.

Ask volunteers to read verses from Psalm 119:1-18, placing special emphasis on verse 9. Say: **If you have ever felt frustrated because you just can't seem to stay away from sin, the Bible is God's single answer for living a pure life. It is more than a book of stories and rules.**

Ask a volunteer to read Romans 1:16 aloud. Then say: **The Bible contains God's powerful plan for drawing people to him and enabling them to live God-pleasing lives.**

Ask: • How does the Bible help us to understand what God is like?

• Why is it so important to read the Word on a regular basis?

• How have you been touched and changed by the Bible?

• What impact has the Bible made in our country? in the world?

• Why do you think the Bible is banned in many countries?

Close with a prayer, asking for passion for God's Word.

Faith Metaphors

Taking It Further

Challenge your teens to read their Bibles daily. Expose them to a Bible reading program, such as those that divide the Bible into daily portions to be read through in a year. For example, see *The Youth Bible,* available from Group Publishing.

The Least of These

The Topic: Caring for others

The Point: Students will learn that God is pleased when we take care of other people.

The Scripture: Matthew 25:34-40

The Object: Tame gerbils or hamsters

The Supplies: You'll need a Bible; gerbils or hamsters, gerbil cages; food; accessories such as water bottles, wood chips, and toys; newspaper; cleaning rags; and a plastic tub of soapy water.

The Object Lesson

Before class, locate some tame gerbils or hamsters by contacting various people in your church. Make sure to ask permission for the animals to be handled during your class time.

Put students to work cleaning the gerbil cages and filling food trays and water bottles. Invite students to gently play with the pets if time allows. They might even try teaching the animals a simple trick.

Ask: • **Do any of you have pets? How do you care for them?**

• **What happens when people neglect their animals?**

• **What sort of needs does an animal have?**

Adapt this object lesson by using whatever pets might be available to you and conducive to your meeting area. Anything goes—dogs, rabbits, cats, earthworms, crickets, or even one of those giant domesticated pigs!

Say: **Just like these animals, people also need food, shelter, and companionship. Oftentimes, those needs go unmet.** Have a volunteer read aloud Matthew 25:34-40.

Ask: • **What is God's plan for taking care of needy people?**

• **How are you caring for Christ by meeting the needs of a person?**

• **How can you reach out to people with emotional needs?**

• **What are some specific needs people in your life are facing?**

• **What are some specific ways you can care for these people?**

Discuss the enjoyment that pets bring. Then remind students of the blessings we receive when we care for other people—reciprocal love, friendship, help in our times of need, and the good feelings that come from obeying God's commands.

Taking It Further

Help students put their good intentions into action by planning a service activity following class time or in the future. Check with local charities or retirement homes for any needs they might have.

What's Inside Counts

The Topic: Character

The Point: Students will learn that God knows what kind of character they have.

The Scripture: 1 Samuel 16:7b

The Object: A box of cereal

The Supplies: You'll need a Bible, one box of cereal, pens, and paper.

The Object Lesson

Have students form pairs or trios, and give each group pens and paper. Hold up a box of cereal.

Say: **Here's *the* greatest box of cereal that ever existed! It is more delicious, more nutritious, and more valuable than any other box of cereal you've ever had! So your group's job is to write a commercial for this box of cereal. Choose a commercial jingle or a Christmas carol you know, and change the words to create a song about this box of cereal.**

Now to sell your cereal, you'll need to let people know just exactly what it is that they're getting. You'll need to come up with the ingredients of the cereal and include those ingredients in your jingle. You'll need to make your ingredients—some pretty yucky things—sound pretty good in your commercials. You might come up with something like "Fortified with wet-sock juice concentrate" or "The dried tree fungus makes you strong!" Have fun with your ingredients, but don't be rude—no bodily functions, please! I'll give you a few minutes to come up with a song.

After everyone has created a commercial, have groups perform their commercials, using the box of cereal as a prop. When everyone is finished, have students form new pairs or trios to discuss these questions:

Ask:
- **Do you look at the ingredients when you buy a box of cereal? Why or why not?**
- **Would you buy this cereal? Why or why not?**
- **What's the point of making a commercial for this box of cereal?**
- **How is making these commercials like the way people judge the character of others?**
- **How can you know what's inside a person's heart?**

Read aloud the cereal's real ingredients to the class. Then open the box of cereal, and let everyone munch on a handful of cereal.

Ask:
- **How are the ingredients you listed for the cereal like or unlike the way we judge someone's character?**
- **How are the real ingredients like or unlike the way God judges someone's character?**

Say: **We often can't or don't "read the ingredients" of people. We might judge people's character by how they look or by what they do. But the good news is that God sees what's on the inside.**

Open the Bible, and read 1 Samuel 16:7b aloud.

Ask: • **What does this Scripture say about our ability to read the "ingredients" of others? of ourselves?**

• **What does this Scripture say about how we should portray ourselves to others?**

Say: **God knows what kinds of character people really have. God knows what's in our hearts. And when we trust in God, we can be confident that our actions reflect our hearts and our character.**

Close by giving handfuls of the cereal as a treat.

Taking It Further

You can use this activity as a "commercial break" for a full-length study on the character of a Bible hero such as Esther, David, or Paul. Break the Bible story you've chosen into two or three segments. Each segment can focus on a certain characteristic that God gave those characters, such as trust, service, love, or humility. Then have groups role-play those segments. Ask another group to conduct the commercials between the segments. During discussion, be sure to talk about how our communication with God is the best way to know the kind of character that honors him.

Choose Life

The Topic: Choices

The Point: Students will learn that God offers life and blessings if we choose to live for him.

The Scripture: Deuteronomy 30:19-20

The Object: Lego toys

The Supplies: You'll need Bibles, Lego toys, and permanent markers.

The Object Lesson

Place several large stacks of Lego toys around the room. Say: **You have thirty seconds to make whatever you want using these construction toys. Go!**

After thirty seconds, allow volunteers to share their creations.

Ask: • Did you choose what you wanted to make first and then build it, or did you start building and then decide what you were making? Why?

• If I gave you another thirty seconds, would you choose to rebuild your structure? Why or why not?

• Suppose you choose to rebuild—how would you build your structure differently?

Hand out Bibles, and ask students to turn to Deuteronomy 30:19-20. Ask the person with the most creative structure to read the passage as others follow along.

Ask: • How are these construction toys like or unlike choices?

• What role do your choices play in the kind of life you lead? Explain.

• How many choices do you think you make in a day?

• How might your choices change if you thought of them as being choices for life or death?

• If your choices changed, how do you think your life would change?

Ask students to form pairs and reread Deuteronomy 30:19-20. Then have them discuss the following questions:

Ask: • According to this passage, what kinds of choices would be choices for life? What kinds of choices would be choices for death?

Prompt students by sharing that reading God's Word daily and having Christian friends would be

FYI

Artists have different methods of creating. Some create a deliberate and detailed plan first, while others go to it and see what happens. Similarly, people "create" their lives either strategically or spontaneously. Your more artistic-minded students might reject the idea that they have to think in black-and-white in order to please God. And they'd be right. However, taking each thought (and choice) captive to the mind of Christ (2 Corinthians 10:5) doesn't hamper creativity; it adds Christ's wisdom.

choices for life. Choices for death might include ditching church right before the sermon or placing more importance on a relationship with a guy or girl than on a relationship with God.

Allow a few people to share what they've discussed.

Ask: • **How do you think your parents' choices have affected you? What effect could your choices as a teenager have on the children you might have someday?**

• **Why is it important to begin choosing life when you're so young?**

Say: **You make hundreds, maybe thousands, of choices each day. Not all of them are earth-shattering, but some may be more important than you know. If you consciously choose to hold fast to God as you make choices, your choices will be wise ones. As a result, God will bless you with a deeper relationship with him.**

FYI

In general, federal copyright laws do not allow you to use videos (even ones you own) for any purpose other than home viewing. Though some exceptions allow for the use of short segments of copyrighted material for educational purposes, it's best to be on the safe side. Your church can obtain a license from the Motion Picture Licensing Corporation for a small fee. Just visit www.mplc.com or call 1-800-462-8855 for more information.

Instruct each student to choose one Lego he or she would like to keep as a reminder of today's lesson. Hand out permanent markers, and ask each person to write "LIFE" on the Lego as a challenge to make choices for God and for life.

Taking It Further

Hand out paper and pens. Ask small groups to brainstorm choices they make each day and label them "life," "death," or "neutral" (a neutral choice would be a choice to wear a turquoise rather than a chartreuse T-shirt).

Show the "Hakuna Matata" scene from Disney's *The Lion King*, and discuss whether the choice to "live only for the present" is a choice for life or death.

Ask small groups to think of a typical high school situation in which a variety of choices would be possible. Give each group an index card and a pen, and ask groups to write their situations on the cards. Collect the cards, shuffle them, and pass them back out. Ask groups to role-play their new situations as others watch. Observers may interrupt the scene by calling out "life" or "death" as they see a choice being made. If they can convince others why they think someone made a life or death choice, they may take over that character's role in the enactment. Continue for a set amount of time or until each situation reaches a resolution.

Signs of Christ

The Topic: Communication

The Point: Students will learn how to let God guide their communication.

The Scripture: Ephesians 4:25, 29, 32; and 5:1-2, 15, 19-21

The Object: Street signs or pictures of street signs

The Supplies: You'll need Bibles, street signs, index cards, pens, and tape.

The Object Lesson

Ask: • **What does it mean to communicate with someone?**

• **What are some important things to remember as you communicate with another person?**

Say: **Let's see what the Bible says about the way God wants us to communicate with each other.** Have a volunteer read aloud Ephesians 4:25, 29, 32; and 5:1-2, 15, 19-21.

Ask: • **What are some of the important principles of communication addressed in this passage?**

Hold up the street signs and encourage students to assign each of the principles, as well as other principles not specifically listed in the passage, to a sign. For example, a speed limit sign might symbolize taking it slow and really listening to someone. An arrow sign might symbolize the need to take the conversation in a different direction. Ask students to write a few words for each sign on index cards and tape them to the signs.

Then have students form pairs. Ask each pair to think of a topic of conversation in which some of these communication principles might come into play.

You might want to give the pairs some of the following topic ideas to get them started.

- A parent and a teenager discussing the use of the family car
- Two friends discussing plans for Saturday night
- A teacher and a teenager discussing the teenager's grade on a recent test
- Two friends discussing a third friend's habits

Have pairs role-play their conversations one at a time. During a conversation, have the rest of the group hold up signs to show what they think needs to happen next in the conversation. For example, if the conversation begins to get heated, someone might hold up a stop sign to symbolize the need to end the conversation and come back to it later when both parties have cooled off.

Taking It Further

Teach a series of lessons to help students identify their own communication styles and issues. Some good resources are *Improving Communication Skills: Interactive Thematic Units for Preventing Conflict* (Teaching and Learning Company), *The Five Love Languages of Children* (Moody Press), and *That's Not What I Meant* (Ballantine Books).

Faith Metaphors

Cold Shoulder

The Topic: Compassion

The Point: Students will learn that in order to be compassionate they need to set aside their own concerns.

The Scripture: Luke 10:30-37

The Object: Ice cubes

The Supplies: You'll need Bibles, a plastic container, two ice cubes for each student, and paper towels.

The Object Lesson

Have students form pairs, and encourage pairs to discuss the following questions:

Ask: • **What is compassion?**

• **Think of news stories you've seen or heard in the past week. Which one stirred compassion in you? Why?**

• **Describe a time someone showed compassion to you. What happened?**

• **What's a compassionate act you've witnessed in the past month?**

Invite partners to share with the whole group any touching stories that emerged during their discussion.

Say: **Compassion is feeling pity or sympathy for someone and then getting involved. Sometimes we can get involved directly. Other times, when we hear about a flood in a distant nation, for example, our involvement might consist of sending money to a relief organization. Compassion always includes some sort of action. It's sympathy with feet under it.**

Ask a volunteer to read aloud Luke 10:30-37.

Ask: • If you wanted to make the same point Jesus made, but use your school as a setting, how would the story go?

• Put yourself in this story. Which character do you think most closely resembles you? Why?

Say: **When we hear this story, we usually think the priest and the Levite walked past the wounded man without caring at all. But Jesus never says that. Maybe the priest didn't want to touch an unclean man and then have to go through purification rituals. Maybe the Levite thought it was a trap and the thieves were still nearby. The priest and the Levite might have been very caring guys who just happened to be too busy to help. They may have felt sympathy—but only the Samaritan had compassion. He set aside his own prejudice and fear and he *acted*. He got involved.**

Ask teenagers to find new partners. Tell pairs they'll now be practicing how to listen compassionately to each other. Compassionate listening is hearing another person with an open and caring heart. Have pairs move away from each other so they can focus without interruption. Tell them they'll have five minutes to discuss the following question:

Ask: • **What's something from your childhood you wish you could change? Why?**

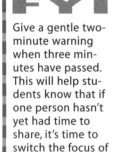

Give a gentle two-minute warning when three minutes have passed. This will help students know that if one person hasn't yet had time to share, it's time to switch the focus of the conversation.

When five minutes is up, thank partners for listening to each other. Tell them they're going to discuss another question for five minutes, but first you have something for them.

Give each teenager an ice cube to hold in one hand throughout the coming five minutes. Explain that the ice cube must be held in the same hand and that the hand should be clenched in a fist.

Ask: • **What's one significant concern you have about your life after graduating from high school?**

When five minutes have passed, give each teenager a paper towel to clean up the water that's melted. Collect what's left of the ice cubes.

Ask: • **How easy or difficult was it to listen compassionately when you had an immediate concern melting in your hand? Why?**

- **How easy or difficult is it for you to put aside your daily concerns and enter compassionately into others' lives? Why?**
- **In what ways has God shown compassion to you?**

Say: **I want to make sure that when you see ice during the coming week, you remember it's important we be compassionate to others. So I've got a special present for each of you: Please pick up your present as you leave the room.**

Have a container of ice cubes by the door. Give each teenager an ice cube as he or she leaves the room.

Taking It Further

Compassion is a way of life, not just a series of laudable acts. Challenge your teenagers to think through how they can engage others compassionately at school, at home, and in other places in their lives. Pray together for a passion for compassion, and commission your teenagers to move through the next week as compassionate ambassadors of God.

You and What Army?

The Topic: Conflict

The Point: Students will learn to handle conflict effectively.

The Scripture: Matthew 5:22-24

The Object: Aspirin

The Supplies: You'll need a Bible and one aspirin tablet for each student.

The Object Lesson

Give each teenager an aspirin tablet.

Say: **I'll need these aspirin tablets back in a few minutes, so please don't drop them or eat them.**

Time for a little history lesson. Aspirin (acetylsalicylic acid) was created in 1897 as a pain reliever by a chemist working for Friedrich Bayer

& Company. But Bayer didn't think aspirin would amount to much. As it turns out, this wasn't a very accurate prediction—according to the Food and Drug Administration, Americans consume an estimated eighty billion aspirin tablets each year.

The pill you hold can help reduce pain, lower fever, and even help some people avoid having heart attacks.

But if you're allergic to aspirin, it can kill you. And even if you're *not* allergic, aspirin can cause nausea, heartburn, and stomach pain. Because aspirin thins your blood, if you have uncontrolled high blood pressure, an ulcer, or liver or kidney disease, the aspirin in your hand can hurt you in serious ways.

Aspirin, like a lot of things, isn't good or bad in itself. It's how you use it that can make aspirin healthy or dangerous, helpful or deadly. What you do with that little tablet makes all the difference.

Ask students to list several items that can be good or bad depending on how they're used. Some examples might include the Internet, cars, jokes, and competition.

Say: **Conflict could be on our list. It's not good or bad—it just *is*. We're all willful, and our goals and desires often don't line up with each others'. That means conflict is inevitable. It's what we *do* with conflict that determines whether it's healthy or dangerous, helpful or deadly.**

Ask a volunteer to read aloud Matthew 5:22-24.

Ask: • **Let's play "Ten Word Summary." How would you sum up what Jesus said in ten words or less?**

• **How do you think people felt when they heard Jesus say this? How do you feel?**

Ask teenagers to form trios and discuss the following questions:

• **Some of us avoid dealing with conflict. What words describe how you feel about conflict?**

• **The words we read from Matthew 5 are Jesus' words. He clearly values the quick resolution of conflicts. Tell about a time you worked through a conflict.**

• **Sometimes we *don't* work through conflicts. What things have kept you from resolving a conflict?**

• **In what ways has conflict been healthy in your life? How has it been unhealthy?**

In their trios, ask students to answer the following questions and then take turns praying for each other.

> • **What is one relationship in which you feel stuck getting through a conflict? What resources do you think might help you?**

Taking It Further

Until your students learn to work through conflict in healthy ways, they'll never have healthy long-term relationships. Explore what the Bible says about conflict resolution, including these passages: Colossians 3:12-14 and Matthew 18:15-16. Have students practice empathic and reflective listening and using "I-statements" to enhance open, honest communication.

Living Sacrifice

The Topic: Conforming to Christ

The Point: Students will learn that they need to conform to the image of Christ.

The Scripture: Romans 12:1-2

The Object: Paper cups

The Supplies: You'll need a Bible, paper cups, markers, paper, and pencils.

The Object Lesson

Have students gather in the center of the meeting room.

> **Ask:** • **What does it mean to conform to something?**
>
> • **What happens when we conform to someone else or his or her ideas?**
>
> • **What happens when we choose not to conform to someone?**

Say: **In many places, the Bible makes it clear that we're to conform to the standard that Christ set. God wants us to be like Christ in everything we think, do, and say. Sin prevents us from accomplishing that, and sin can cause us to conform to a sinful standard.**

Hold up a paper cup, and explain that the cup represents humans. Give the cup to one student, and ask him or her to name one sin that many teenagers commit. After the student names the sin, instruct him or her to crush the cup just a little bit. Repeat this with each student, asking each one to name a sin and crush the cup a little bit. When you're finished, the cup should be completely crushed. Hold the cup up so everyone can see it.

Say: **I'd like you to look at what our lives look like without Christ's control.**

Ask: • **What's the end result of a life that's full of sin?**

• **Why do some people choose to live like this?**

Read Romans 12:1-2 aloud to students.

Ask: • **What does it mean to be a living sacrifice?**

• **Why is it important for a sacrifice to be acceptable to God?**

• **What makes a sacrifice acceptable?**

• **How can we be living sacrifices?**

Hold up an uncrumpled cup. Explain to students that the cup is like Christ. It's perfect and unaffected by sin. Then hold up the cup students helped destroy.

Ask: • **What do I need to do to make this ruined cup get back to its original shape?**

Allow students to share their answers. Then slowly slide the destroyed cup over the good one, forcing the crushed cup to conform to the good cup.

Ask: • **What just happened? Explain.**

Say: **Being a living sacrifice isn't easy. When we conform to Christ, we're sacrificing ourselves. The process to become a living sacrifice isn't easy, and it's often painful. But it's essential as we conform to Christ.**

FYI

You might want to use a plastic cup instead of a second paper cup. The plastic cup is less likely to bend, and it's an excellent contrast with the paper cup.

Have students get in pairs. Ask pairs to brainstorm ways they can conform to the image Christ set before them in Scripture. After one minute, ask each pair to choose its best idea and choose a representative to come forward and write the idea on the uncrumpled paper cup. When the ideas have been written on the cup, read each idea aloud.

Say: **I'd like you to choose one area of your life that doesn't conform to Christ's life. You might choose one of the things that we listed on the cup or something else. I'll give you a minute to think.**

Allow students to pray silently as they think about areas of their lives that don't conform to Christ.

Say: **I'd like you to make a commitment today to let Christ have this area of your life and allow him to conform you more to him.**

Distribute slips of paper and pencils. Ask students to write the areas they want to give to Christ on the slips of paper. When students are finished, have them fold their papers. Pass the perfect cup around, and ask students to place their papers in the cup. Ask a few students to pray for the group.

Taking It Further

To help students understand the Old Testament concept of sacrifice, prepare a teaching about the Old Testament sacrificial system.

New Creations

The Topic: Creation

The Point: Students will learn that believing in Jesus makes us new creations.

The Scripture: 2 Corinthians 5:17

The Object: Clay

The Supplies: You'll need Bibles, clay, sequins, small beads, yarn, and chenille wires.

The Object Lesson

Give each student a large lump of clay. Set out the other supplies where students can share them.

Say: **God created each of us to be unique individuals. He formed our bodies, giving each of us our own unique features. With your clay, I'd like you to form a representation of the way you look.**

Give students several minutes to form their shapes. Then go around the room, and let each person introduce and explain his or her clay figure.

Say: **All of our outward characteristics—the way we look—came from God. God created each of us. That in itself is miraculous. But there's much more to our creation than how we look. I'll show you what I mean.**

Have students look up 2 Corinthians 5:17. Ask a volunteer to read the verse aloud as others follow along in their Bibles.

Ask: • **What do you think this verse means?**

• **What kinds of changes take place when we become new creations in Christ?**

Say: **The clay figure you made earlier represented your original creation—how God made you physically. But when we believe in Jesus, we become new creations on the inside. Use your clay to make something that represents how belief in Jesus changes you on the inside. For example, maybe you'll make a heart shape to represent that believing in Jesus changes your heart. Or maybe you'll make a smile to show that believing in Jesus brings joy to your life.**

Give students several minutes to form their new creations. Then have students form pairs to answer the following questions. Invite volunteers to share their answers with the rest of the class.

Ask: • **How was your second clay creation different from your first?**

• **How is that like how you become a new creation when you believe in Jesus?**

Say: **When we believe in Jesus, he changes us from the inside out. We're new creations. Take these clay creations home with you to remind you that, because of Jesus, you're a new creation!**

Taking It Further

Have students each draw a line down the center of a sheet of paper. (If your students have journals in class, suggest that they do this exercise in their journals so they can refer to it later.) On the left side of the paper, have students write or draw characteristics they had before becoming to believe in Jesus. On the right side of the paper, have them write or draw how believing in Jesus has changed them and made them new creations.

Father Knows Best

The Topic: Dating

The Point: Students will learn that God knows what's best for them in their dating relationships.

The Scripture: Proverbs 3:5-6

The Object: A telephone book

The Supplies: You'll need Bibles, a telephone book for every two or three students, paper, and pens.

The Object Lesson

Have students form same-sex pairs. If you have an uneven number of boys or girls, let students form a trio. Give each group a telephone book, and give each person a pen and paper.

Say: **Let's talk about a subject I'm sure will be interesting to you—dating! In your group, take turns opening your phone book at random and choosing a name. You can choose from either the white pages or the yellow pages, but your choice must be random. The name you choose should be of someone of the opposite sex and someone you don't know.**

Then, on your paper, draw a face to go with the name you chose. Draw what you think someone you would like to date might look like. After you've drawn the picture, write a list of characteristics this dream date might have. You must base at least part of your list from information you've gathered from the phone book.

For example, where does your person live? Does that give you a clue as to whether your person is wealthy or not? What kind of name does he or she have, and what can you tell from that? If you've chosen a name from the yellow pages, what can you tell from the person's occupation? For instance, what kind of education do you think the person has? How important is that to you? The rest of your list can be based on personal preference, but you may include only two or three characteristics based on information not found in the phone book.

Give students about five minutes to choose the names, draw the pictures, and write the lists. Then invite each student to hold up his or her drawing and describe the dream date to the rest of the class. Make sure students explain which information they deduced from the phone book.

Next, have students discuss the following questions in their groups. After each question, invite volunteers to share their answers with the rest of the class.

Ask: • **How was choosing a name from the phone book like looking for someone to date in a big school or community?**

• **Was it easy or difficult to know about the person whose name you chose from the phone book? Explain.**

• **How is that like dating someone you really don't know?**

• **What kinds of things could go wrong when you choose someone to date using the "phone book" approach?**

• **How many items on your dream date list were based on outward characteristics, such as looks, popularity, or money?**

• **In your experience, how is that like the way people in real life choose someone to date?**

Say: **Unfortunately, people often choose someone to date based on superficial characteristics. They may want to go out with someone from the popular crowd, or someone with money, or someone with a nice car, or someone who's a cheerleader, or someone who's good looking. Look at your list again.**

Ask: • **Which of the characteristics you wrote would be important if you were upset and needed to talk? If you were sick or hurt?**

• **Can you tell from your list how your dream date might act if he or she were tempted to cheat on a test or steal from a store? Why or why not?**

• **What will your dream date do if he or she gets angry with you?**

• **Which of the characteristics on your dream date's list would help you grow closer to God?**

Say: **As I said, we often base our date choices on superficial characteristics, which don't mean a thing when a problem arises. But even when we base our choices on inward characteristics, we still have no way of knowing what decisions our date might make or how he or she would respond in certain situations. It's almost like choosing a name at random from a phone book. We can't know another person's heart or what will happen in the future. But God knows. Let's look at a few verses that give us direction.**

Have groups look up and read Proverbs 3:5-6.

Ask: • **What do these verses tell us?**

• **How can these Scriptures help you make wise choices about who you date?**

Say: **God knows our hearts, and he knows what will happen in the future. If we trust our lives to him, he'll protect us from harmful relationships and direct us where he wants us to be. Let's do that right now.**

Have students pray with their partners, asking God to direct their steps.

Taking It Further

If you think your students would be comfortable, ask volunteers to share (without naming names) dating experiences that would have been more successful had they asked God to be in control. From there, you could lead into an entire lesson on trusting God with all aspects of life.

Do You Trust Me?

The Topic: Death

The Point: Students will learn that they can trust God to care for them after they die.

The Scripture: John 14:1-6

The Object: An ultrasound picture

The Supplies: You'll need Bibles, one ultrasound picture for each trio of teenagers (photocopies work well), a stopwatch or a watch with a second hand, and markers.

The Object Lesson

Have students form trios.

Say: **It's been said that you only have to do two things in life: pay taxes and die. But there *is* a third thing: you also have to be born.**

Give each trio an ultrasound picture.

Say: **Just in case you don't know, the picture you're holding is an ultrasound image. It is a picture of a fetus created by sending high-frequency sound waves into a woman's body and then detecting reflected sound waves and creating a graphic representation of them. It's sort of a spy-cam aimed at an unborn baby.**

As a trio, decide on a name for your new friend in the ultrasound image. You've got thirty seconds.

Ask trios to volunteer what they named their ultrasound pictures and why.

Say: **I'm glad you bonded with your new friends so well because now it's time to have a little chat with them. Let's assume your friends are about to be born. In just twelve hours, they'll emerge into a world they've never experienced—the "outside" world. Your job is to describe our outside world in a way someone in your baby's situation will understand, including what they're about to experience as they're born. Remember: Your baby has never taken a breath, never** seen light, never eaten, and never been outside the womb. You've got five minutes to bring your baby up to speed. Go for it.

Tell groups when they have thirty seconds left. Ask trios to share some of the things they decided to say.

Say: *Very* informative—but I think your babies are still in for a shock. No matter how hard we try, it's almost impossible to explain something that another person has never experienced. There's no frame of reference, no words that connect. The biggest question a thinking baby might ask is, "Is there someone out there I can trust to catch me and care for me?" If so, everything will be fine. If not, nothing's going to save the baby.

It would make perfect sense for a baby to be *terrified* of being born—it's a forced journey into the unknown.

One day you, too, will be launched onto a journey into the unknown: the experience of dying. In your trios, I'd like you to discuss the following questions:

Ask: • In what ways is the process of dying like the process of being born?

• If you could have any one piece of information about dying, what would it be?

• When you think about dying, do you feel hopeful or hopeless? Why?

After trios talk together, invite them to share insights from their discussions with the larger group.

Say: **Jesus answered a lot of questions in great detail. But when he talked about death and what comes after it, Jesus wasn't very specific. Listen to what he told his disciples about dying.**

Ask a volunteer to read aloud John 14:1-6.

Ask: • Exactly what do you think Jesus was saying in this passage?

• If you're a follower of Jesus, how does hearing these words Jesus shared with his followers make you feel? Why?

Say: **Jesus didn't give details. Explaining the reality of life after physical death to his disciples—and us—must be like our explaining the "outside" world to a baby.**

Instead, Jesus assures us that someone we can trust is there to catch us and care for us. We can trust God. We can trust Jesus. We don't have to let our hearts be troubled.

Invite trios to write reassuring words on their ultrasound pictures. Collect the pictures and post them in a prominent spot in the room.

Taking It Further

This devotion is a good launching pad for exploring what the Bible says about being in a relationship with God through Jesus. It's also an appropriate introduction to a study of how Jesus faced physical death with absolute trust in God (Luke 23:38-46) and how Stephen faced death at the hands of an angry crowd (Acts 6:8–7:1, 54-60).

Sitting on the Sidelines

The Topic: Drugs and alcohol

The Point: Students will learn that those who abuse drugs and alcohol can't serve God effectively.

The Scripture: Ephesians 5:17-20

The Object: A rubber band

The Supplies: You'll need Bibles, and the following objects for each student: one penny, one steel or brass washer, and six large rubber bands.

The Object Lesson

Give each student a penny.

Say: **Now it's time to try a little dexterity experiment. No college scholarships hang in the balance, so don't stress. The goal is to flip the penny in the air with one hand and catch it with your other hand. Hang time isn't important—just get it done. Everyone try.**

Allow teenagers to try several times. If some students aren't able to flip the coins, let them just toss the coins in the air with one hand and catch them with the other.

Say: **Congratulations! You are now all semipro flipper-catchers. Your job is to be available at any time to flip a penny in the air with one hand and catch it with the other hand.**

Let's say that you're on call right now, but things are quiet on the flipper-catcher front, so you decide to relax with a couple of beers. Your blood-alcohol content is affected a bit.

When your blood-alcohol content reaches .02 to .04, your mood is intensified and your memory and judgment are slightly impaired.

Give each student six rubber bands, and ask each student to slip one rubber band over his or her hands, fastening the hands together palm-to-palm. Then ask students to try flipping and catching their pennies.

Say: **Looks like your ability to do your job is compromised a bit—but not much. So you have another beer, and your blood-alcohol level rises to about .05. You're now experiencing a slight balance and speech disturbance. Slip on another rubber band and try doing your flip-catch job again.**

Have each student put another rubber band around his or her hands and try to flip and catch.

Say: **Time for some more beer. When your blood-alcohol level is between .07 and .13, your reaction time is significantly reduced. Your judgment is seriously impaired. Slip on two more rubber bands, and try doing your flip-catch job again.**

After teenagers try, say: **A few more drinks, and you're at a blood-alcohol level of .18 to .30. You're generally confused and hazy now, and all your cognitive abilities are disrupted. Slide on the other rubber bands, and give flipping-catching a try. Not easy, is it?**

Ask teenagers to remove the rubber bands, form trios, and discuss these questions.

Ask: • **How easy or difficult was it to do your job when rubber bands were added to your hands?**

• **In what ways have you seen alcohol or drugs affect people?**

• **What would you say to someone who says it's OK to get drunk? What would you say to someone who says it's never OK to drink alcohol?**

Ask teenagers to share insights from their discussions. Then ask a volunteer to read aloud Ephesians 5:17-20.

Ask: • **Picture getting this advice from your parents— would you consider it good advice or lame advice? Why?**

• **What does this passage say about consuming alcohol? If you were writing a rule, how would you sum up what you see in this passage?**

Say: **There are lots of good reasons to avoid getting drunk or stoned, and here's a good one: When you abuse alcohol or drugs, you can't take advantage of opportunities to serve God. You're like a flipper-catcher who has rubber-banded his or her hands together.**

Ask: • **What sort of opportunities to serve God might you miss if you're abusing alcohol or drugs?**

• **What does abusing alcohol or drugs communicate about your spiritual life?**

• **What advice would you give someone who was abusing alcohol or drugs?**

Give each student a washer.

Say: **In most hospitals, doctors who are "on call"—ready and waiting to respond to a patient's needs—wear pagers. I couldn't afford pagers, but I could afford washers. Please place the washer I gave you in your change purse or in a pocket where you keep your change. When you stumble across it while sorting through your change, let it remind you that you're on-call at all times to serve God. Decide now not to do anything that would compromise your effectiveness—and that includes abusing alcohol or drugs.**

Taking It Further

Invite a health-care provider or representative of your community's Alcoholics Anonymous program to visit and discuss the risks associated with drug or alcohol abuse, or do an in-depth study of what the Bible says about consuming alcohol.

The Strength of the Lord

The Topic: Encouragement

The Point: Students will learn the true meaning of encouragement.

The Scripture: 1 Samuel 23:7-18

The Object: A barbell with heavy weights

The Supplies: You'll need Bibles and a barbell with heavy weights.

The Object Lesson

Have someone help you set the barbell in front of the group.

Say: **I have a really heavy weight here. Do any of you think you could lift it? Raise your hand if you think you can lift this weight.**

Let those who raised their hands come up and try to lift the weight.

Say: **This weight is too heavy to lift by yourself.**

Ask: • **How is this weight like a really difficult problem?**

• **What kinds of heavy weights—difficult problems—have you had to lift?**

• **What helped you lift those weights?**

Say: **Let's hear a story from David's life. He was lifting a really heavy weight—one that was much too heavy for him to lift alone.**

Ask a volunteer to read 1 Samuel 23:7-15 aloud.

Ask: • **What "weight" was David lifting?**

• **Why do you think his weight was so hard to handle?**

Make sure the barbell is holding enough weight that no one person in your group could lift it. It'll need to be light enough so that your whole group could lift it, however. If you have athletes in your group, you'll need to plan accordingly.

Throughout this exercise, practice good spotting techniques to ensure everyone's safety. You may need to have a few other strong adults on hand to help.

Say: **Saul used to be David's friend, but he now wanted to kill him. David was running from Saul. He had to have felt very alone and betrayed.**

Ask: • **What might have helped David?**

Have a volunteer read aloud 1 Samuel 23:16-18.

Say: **David's friend Jonathan came to David and encouraged him by helping him find strength in God. This is what true encouragement looks like—helping someone to find strength in God.**

Encourage students to work together to lift the barbell.

Say: **Just as you helped each other find the strength to lift the barbell, Jonathan helped David find the strength in God to help him carry on through a difficult time.**

Ask: • **What are some ways you could help others find strength in God?**

Say: **When we encourage others through tough times, we can help them find strength in God that will help them to carry on.**

Taking It Further

Extend this object lesson by having students identify specific people in their own lives who they could offer encouragement to and specific ways they could show encouragement. Ask students to commit to doing at least one act of encouragement during the next week and then report back to the group the following week. Ask students how it felt to encourage others in this way.

As Far as the East Is From the West...

The Topic: Failure

The Point: Students will learn God's view of their failures and sins.

The Scripture: Psalm 103:8-12

The Object: Binoculars

The Supplies: You'll need Bibles, binoculars, newsprint, a marker, and tape.

The Object Lesson

Draw and color in a large black dot on a sheet of newsprint, and hang it on one wall.

Ask: • **Have you ever failed at anything? Explain.**

• **How did you feel when you failed?**

Say: **When we fail at something, it may seem like a big black dot on a white page.** Give a volunteer the binoculars, and ask him or her to look through them at the dot. Say: **We may feel as if our failures are really big. The more we think about them, the bigger they seem, in the same way that these binoculars make the dot look bigger.** Give each person a chance to look at the dot through the binoculars.

Ask: • **How do you think God views our failures?**

Have a volunteer read Psalm 103:8-12.

Ask: • **What do these verses tell us God does with our transgressions, or failures?**

• **Why do you think God views our failures in this way?**

Give a volunteer the binoculars, and have him or her turn them around backward and look through them at the dot. Give each person a chance to look at the dot this way.

Say: **Even though we may see our failures magnified, God sees them as very small. In fact, he removes them from us completely. He does** this because he loves us too much to let us be bogged down and overwhelmed by our sins and failures. What a great God!

Taking It Further

Study people in the Bible who have failed in really big ways and yet God turned their failures around and used them in big ways to further his kingdom. Some examples are Paul (Acts 9) and David (1 and 2 Samuel).

Use It or Lose It

The Topic: Faith

The Point: Students will learn that faith develops through use.

The Scripture: 1 Corinthians 9:24-27

The Object: A jump rope

The Supplies: You'll need Bibles and jump ropes.

The Object Lesson

Ask students to share ways they keep their bodies in shape. Then set out jump ropes, and give everyone a chance to use the jump ropes to exercise. Encourage teenagers to use the jump ropes in different ways. For example, a person could rotate the rope and jump over it. Or two people could hold either end of a rope, one person could sit on the ground, and the other person could pull the partner up. Or two people could hold either end of a rope and pull with their arm muscles in opposite directions. Encourage youth to be creative in developing new exercises with the ropes.

After everyone has had a chance to exercise, have students sit together for a discussion.

Ask: • **What would happen to your muscles if you used a jump rope several times a day, every day?**

FYI

If you don't have jump ropes, you can use any exercise equipment you can find. You can use thick rubber bands to work upper-body and lower-body muscles, lift heavy items like jugs of water, climb stairs, and so on.

- **What would happen to your muscles if you quit using the jump rope for weeks and weeks?**

Say: **In order to grow strength in your muscles, you've got to use them. Muscles aren't the only things that require work to grow.**

Have students open their Bibles to 1 Corinthians 9:24-27, and follow along as a volunteer reads aloud the Scripture.

Ask: • **What do you think is meant by "a crown that will last forever"?**

- **How is running aimlessly different from what is required in order for us to receive this crown?**

- **How is building faith like building muscle?**

- **What kind of exercises could you do to build your faith?**

Have students form groups of three or four. Ask each group to develop an exercise people can use to build their faith. For example, a group might suggest answering another person's questions about Jesus, keeping a prayer journal, or actively seeking out answers to questions that can cause spiritual doubt.

After three or four minutes, have each group take a turn explaining its exercise to the larger group. Then ask each person to decide which exercise he or she would like to try. Give students about five minutes to exercise their faith using an exercise a group explained.

Ask: • **What are some of the risks of working out our muscles?**

- **What are some of the risks of working out our faith?**

- **How can you overcome those risks or fear of those risks?**

- **What are the benefits of working out muscles?**

- **What are the benefits of working out faith?**

- **Do the benefits of developing faith outweigh the risks? Explain.**

Say: **The Bible acknowledges that living out our faith can be difficult. Faith isn't something that just happens. We have to work at it. We have to exercise. We have to use it to grow it.**

Taking It Further

Have students get back into their groups of three or four. Assign each group a segment of Hebrews 11 to read. Then have each group discuss how the faith was developed by the person or people identified in the segment of Scripture. Ask members of each group to share what they learned with the larger group. Have each person create a weekly plan to exercise faith, based on Scripture and the exercises the groups created.

Family Matters

The Topic: Family

The Point: Students will learn that God wants us to show love to our family members.

The Scripture: 1 John 4:7-11

The Object: A rubber ball

The Supplies: You'll need Bibles, a rubber ball for every two or three students, and double-sided tape.

The Object Lesson

Ask: • **Has anyone here ever had a disagreement with a family member? Let's see a show of hands.**

• **Has anyone here ever said something mean to a family member that you wouldn't say to your friends? Raise your hand if you have.**

Say: **There's an old saying that says, "You only hurt the ones you love." We sometimes tend to act our very worst around those who love us the most—our family members. And they sometimes act the same way toward us. Let's see what that's like. Think of the disagreements you sometimes have with your parents or siblings. Think of one thing you've said recently that you regret.**

Have students sit in a large circle on the floor. (An uncarpeted floor works best for this activity.) Place all but one ball in the center of the circle.

Hand the remaining ball to a volunteer. Have the volunteer repeat the statement he or she thought of and roll the ball into the group of other balls. Then have kids quickly regroup the balls in the middle of the circle.

Have the next person in the circle reach the closest ball and repeat the process, rolling the ball at the group of balls. After everyone has repeated a statement and rolled a ball, gather the balls together in the middle of the circle.

Have students each turn to a partner to answer the following questions. After each question, invite partners to share their answers with the rest of the class.

Ask: • **How might the group of balls in the middle of the circle be like your family?**

• **How is the ball you rolled like saying or doing an unkind thing to someone in your family?**

• **What happened to the group of balls in the center of the circle when another ball hit them?**

• **How is that like what happens when we say or do unkind things to our family members?**

Say: **Just as the group of balls moved apart when they were hit, when we hit a family member with an unkind word or deed, we break the family apart a little bit. But that's not what God wants.**

Have students turn to 1 John 4:7-11. Ask a volunteer to read the passage aloud as others follow along in their Bibles.

Ask: • **What does this passage have to say about how we should treat our family members?**

• **What happens in a family when we show love?**

Wrap double-sided tape around a ball.

Say: **When we're unkind to our family members, we break the family apart, just as the group of balls were broken apart. But when we show love, we bind the family together. Think of one way you can show love to a family member this week. Maybe you'll compliment your brother, or tell your mother how much you appreciate what she does for you.**

Hand the taped ball to a volunteer in the circle. Have the volunteer say the way he or she will show love to a family member this week, then roll the taped ball into the middle of the circle.

Ask: • **What happened this time when you rolled the ball into the circle?**

• **How is that like what can happen when we show love to our family members?**

Say: **Just as the taped ball stuck to the other balls, showing love helps a family stick together, instead of breaking it apart. Let's ask God to help us treat our families with the love he shows us.**

Close in prayer, asking for God's help in showing love to our family members.

Taking It Further

Have students identify recurring problems they have with family members, then have them research Scripture passages that deal with those problems. Finally, have student compose scripts and role-play possible solutions to the problems they've been having at home.

Our Many-Colored Group

The Topic: Feelings

The Point: Students will learn that God wants to speak to them about their feelings.

The Scripture: Hebrews 4:12-13

The Object: Sidewalk chalk

The Supplies: You'll need a Bible and sidewalk chalk.

The Object Lesson

Set out several pieces of colored sidewalk chalk, and ask each student to choose a color to represent himself or herself.

Take the group outside. Instruct a volunteer to use his or her chalk to draw a line, squiggle, or shape. Then have the volunteer choose another person to

draw another line that somehow interacts with the first line. Continue until everyone has made a mark. Allow the group to be seated around their masterpiece.

Ask: • **What do you think of our drawing?**

• **How do the various lines work together?**

• **Would our drawing be more or less interesting if it had fewer squiggles and lines? Explain.**

• **How are the colors of your chalk similar to feelings?**

• **What kind of marks do feelings make on our lives that might be like the chalk marks on the ground?**

• **How do you most often express your feelings?**

FYI

If you have more students than chalk, you'll need to divide pieces until everyone has some.

FYI

If it isn't possible to go outside, provide newsprint, and do the activity inside.

Say: **Feelings make life more colorful and interesting, just like the way our different colors of chalk make our drawing more interesting. God created feelings as an important part of who we are as people.**

Ask students to form pairs and discuss these questions:

Ask: • **Why did you choose the color you did?**

• **Do you feel good about your choice? If not, which piece would you prefer to represent you?**

Gather the group back together and read aloud Hebrews 4:12-13.

Say: **God already knows how you feel, and God's Word has something to say about your feelings, or "the attitudes of the heart." As you read** the Bible and allow God to speak to you through his Word, he can encourage you, give you peace, or tell you what you need to know or do in order to feel differently.

Challenge students to go to God with their feelings and see what a difference God can make.

Taking It Further

Read aloud Dr. Seuss' *My Many Colored Days*. Ask questions like: "Do you relate to this book? Why or why not?" "Does one color represent you most often? If so, which one and why?"

Provide strips of dark-colored construction paper. Allow students to make Bible bookmarks with their chalk (perhaps featuring Hebrews 4:12-13) to remind them to take their feelings to God and listen for what his Word has to say.

Grappling With Guidance

The Topic: Following God

The Point: Students will learn that God's plan for their lives may not always be clear, but they can always trust him to be faithful.

The Scripture: Exodus 13:17-22; Jeremiah 29:11-13

The Object: A cellular phone

The Supplies: You'll need a Bible, six to eight cellular phones, pens, and sticky notes.

The Object Lesson

Write each phone number on a sticky note, and put it on the phone it belongs to. Hide the phones throughout the building you are meeting in. After you hide a phone, take off the sticky note and write down where the phone is located. Keep the sticky notes for later use. After all the phones have been hidden and you have collected all the sticky notes, you are ready to begin.

Find a room with a phone other than your usual meeting room. Dial the number of the phone in your meeting room, and explain the activity to the student who answers the phone. Say: **This is a cell-phone scavenger hunt. Follow the ringing until you find the location of the next phone. Answer it, and I will give you further details.**

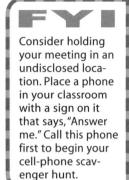

Give students a simple clue over the phone to help them narrow down the vicinity of their next phone. Then dial the second phone you want them to locate. When students find and answer the phone, give them a clue to help them locate the third phone. Continue until students have found all of the phones. Be sure they are collecting the phones along the way so they can be returned to you at the conclusion of the activity. When students locate the last phone, give them a clue as to where you are, and ask them to join you.

Say: **Wouldn't it be nice if hearing God's voice was as simple as picking up a phone and awaiting further instructions? Even when we try to reach God, it can feel as if he's not answering or we're getting a busy signal—or maybe we feel there is just so much static on the line, and we can't make sense of what he is trying to tell us.**

Following God can feel like a wild chase. We don't really know where we're going, and deciphering his will can be really tricky. Sometimes God may lead us through difficult places we would rather avoid. And some of the things he asks of us may seem to make no sense. But throughout the history of God's people, those who follow God have felt this way at times. We can learn from their stories that we can trust God to be faithful to us during our journeys just as he was faithful through other people's journeys. Ask a volunteer to read Exodus 13:17-22 aloud.

Ask: • **Why do you think God led his people along a more difficult path than was necessary?**

• **Can you describe a time when God led you through a difficulty that might have been avoided?**

• **How does God guide us in the path he wants us to follow?**

Say: **You might remember how the story ended. The people grumbled,** mistrusted, disobeyed, and were punished. God led them around aimlessly for forty years. It was a new generation that actually enjoyed the land God had promised.

Ask: • How might the people's journey have been different if they had faithfully followed God's leading?

• What sort of problems do we encounter when we refuse to follow God's leading?

• What blessings do we enjoy when we do what God asks us to?

Close by reading Jeremiah 29:11-13 aloud.

Taking It Further

Use this lesson to serve as a springboard into discussion about how to know the will of God. Explain to students that the Bible is like a road map, giving us the directions that God wants us to follow. Have students search through the Scriptures and compile a "To Do" list of commands from the Bible. Explain that we are in line with God's will when we are following the instructions he has given. Micah 6:8 and James 1:27 would be good verses for students with.

Laying Down the Burden of Unforgiveness

The Topic: Forgiveness

The Point: Students will learn that unforgiveness places a harmful burden on us that only forgiveness can lift.

The Scripture: Ephesians 4:30-32

The Object: Canned goods

The Supplies: You'll need Bibles, an empty pillowcase, and ten to fifteen pounds of canned goods.

The Object Lesson

Give each person a can or two, and have students stand in a circle facing each other. Place the pillowcase in the middle of the circle. Have students hold the items straight out in front of them throughout the following discussion. As students respond, encourage them to give examples of the effects of unforgiveness they've observed or experienced.

Ask: • **What does the word "unforgiveness" mean to you?**

• **How is holding on to unforgiveness like carrying a weight or burden?**

• **What are some examples of bad things we can experience or cause others to experience when we refuse to forgive?**

Have students keep holding the cans up for the entire time as they share. When all are finished, have students place the cans in the pillowcase and pass the full bag around the circle so everyone feels the weight for several seconds. Keep holding the bag as you lead the following discussion.

Read Ephesians 4:30-32 aloud.

Ask: • **How is being bitter, angry, or slanderous like carrying a heavy burden?**

• **How can being kind, compassionate, and forgiving relieve us of this burden?**

• **Why do you think it is so important to God that we be kind, compassionate, and forgiving instead of bitter and angry?**

Say: **If we refuse to forgive those who hurt us or who do wrong to us, we will end up carrying quite a burden, causing harm to both ourselves and those we've refused to forgive.**

Ask: • **From what people shared earlier, what kinds of things did the cans in this pillowcase represent?**

• **How would your life be affected if you carried this pillowcase full of canned goods around with you every minute of every day?**

• **How can carrying these kinds of things around inside us—practicing them as part of our regular**

behavior or letting them affect our attitudes—
become like a burden to us, weighing us down?

Say: **Whew! These things get really heavy after we carry them around for a while.**

Place the bag in the middle of the circle again.

Say: **Some of us are carrying around a pretty hefty burden of unforgiveness, bitterness, and anger. Just as I placed this burden on the ground, some of us need to get out from under our burden and let Christ's love flow all over our hearts and lives.**

Ask: • **What will it take for us to forgive as Christ forgave?**

Allow students time to be alone and reflect on any unforgiveness they may hold in their hearts toward others. Emphasize that when we forgive someone, we end our anger toward them. We give up any resentment in our heart toward the person. We neutralize the desire to punish them and give up all claim to penalize them. We offer them grace in love—a way out—just as Christ gave us grace, loved us, and gave us a way out of penalty and punishment for our sin. Close by leading the group in prayer to forgive those toward whom they hold unforgiveness. Take cues for your prayer from the responses of students to the last question you asked them.

Taking It Further

If you're short on time, simply fill the pillowcase with cans, and leave out the part where students hold the cans out in front of them. The discussion will still work well.

A celebration of the Lord's Supper would be very appropriate to add to the end of this activity. It would provide a great opportunity for students to patch up relationships. It would also allow them an opportunity to express thanksgiving and worship to Christ for carrying the weight of the world's sin on himself on the cross. It may be appropriate to read Matthew 19:26 to students who are struggling to forgive others to remind them that with God's help, they can forgive.

No Greater Love

The Topic: Friendship

The Point: Students will learn that Jesus' love for us is the true meaning of friendship.

The Scripture: John 15:12-13

The Object: Clothespins

The Supplies: You'll need a Bible, three clothespins for each student, one paper lunch bag for every three or four students, and fine-point markers.

The Object Lesson

Have students form groups of three or four. Give each student two clothespins, and give each group one lunch bag. Have groups open their lunch bags and place them in the middle of the groups. Hand out markers.

Say: **You each should have two clothespins. Take a minute to think of a good friend you have. On one clothespin, write one word that describes your friendship with that person. Don't let anyone see what you write.**

Give students a few seconds to write, and ask students to place in their groups' bags the clothespins they just wrote on.

Say: **Now on your other clothespin, write a word that describes someone who may not be so friendly to you.**

Give students a few seconds to write on their clothespins, and ask students to place the clothespins in their groups' bags.

Tell students to take turns pulling clothespins out of their groups' bags and clipping the clothespins to their shirts. It's OK if one person has either two negative descriptions or two positive descriptions. Have everyone continue until each student has two clothespins pinned to his or her shirt. Have groups discuss these questions.

Ask: • **Do you like the descriptions you are pinned to? Why or why not?**

- **Do you think it's fair that you are labeled that way? Why or why not?**

- **How will people treat you based on the descriptions that have been pinned to you?**

Have each student take one of the clothespins and clip it to both his or her shirt and to the shirt of the person sitting at the left. Have them repeat with the other clothespin, clipping it to his or her shirt and to the shirt of the person sitting at the right.

Ask: • **How would you react to the people who are clipped to you if they acted the way their clothespins say?**

• **How is that similar to how you might react to your friends if they acted the same way? How is it different?**

Have a volunteer read John 15:12-13 aloud.

Ask: • **Does this Scripture change the way you might react to the person you are clipped to? Explain.**

• **The Scripture says to love each other as Jesus loves us. How can we do that?**

Say: **Jesus was talking about his love in this Scripture. There is no greater love than loving others the way Jesus loves us. The love can be as big as saving someone's life, but it can also be as small as being** nice to another person, even if that person is not nice to you. What's so great about this Scripture is that not only does it tell us how great Jesus' love is, it tells us that we, too, can be instruments of that love by the way we are "clipped" to our friends.

Distribute another clothespin to each student, and ask students to write "John 15:12-13" on one side of the clothespin. Challenge students to keep the clothespins clipped to their clothes for the rest of the day until they can clip the clothespins onto friends—perhaps without the friends knowing!

Taking It Further

You can use this lesson as an attention-getting opener to a lesson on the parable of the vine and the branches, found in John 15:1-17. Distribute several strands of green yarn to students, and tell them to think about how their relationships with Jesus changes aspects of their lives.

Begin a "vine" by taping several strands of yarn to a wall near the ceiling. While you're reading and discussing the parable, ask students to get up and add a strand of yarn to the vine for every one of those life-changing aspects as they think of them. Include a closing activity in which everyone adds at least one strand. Then encourage students to clip their clothespins to the vine as the fruit—as reminders to offer to their friends the love that Jesus has shared with them.

God's Love Never Lets Go

The Topic: God's love

The Point: Students will learn that God's love is a permanent bond that never lets us go.

The Scripture: Romans 8:35-39

The Object: Super glue

The Supplies: You'll need Bibles, super glue, items that can be glued together, and two identical items that have been glued together.

The Object Lesson

Hold up the items you glued together for students to see. Have students take turns trying to pull the items apart. Then display the identical items that are not glued together. Press the items together but show how they just do not stay together.

Say: **These items are separate until they are joined together with glue. This glue establishes a bond that cannot be broken by us.**

Ask: • **How is this glue like God's love for us? Explain.**

Read Romans 8:35-39 aloud.

Ask: • **What does this passage tell us about God's love?**

• **Why is this so important for us to know?**

• **How does it make you feel to know that nothing can separate you from God's love? Explain.**

• **When have you experienced God's "never-lets-go" kind of love?**

Have students form small groups of three or four. In their small groups, have students discuss the following questions:

Ask: • **Tell of a time you doubted God's love, a time you thought God had given up on you, or a time you could not feel God's love.**

• **In what ways do you struggle to believe in or feel God's never-lets-go love? Explain.**

• **How can we remind one another of God's never-lets-go kind of love?**

After students have shared in their small groups, have them pray for each other according to what each shared. Close in prayer, thanking God for his never-lets-go love.

Consider gluing items together for each group member as reminders of God's never-lets-go love.

Taking It Further

To expand this into a study, consider having students come up with examples of ways people in the Bible experienced God's never-lets-go love.

As a closing application, have students role-play helping one another go through tough times and believe in God's never-lets-go kind of love (such as after suffering a tragedy like a crippling car accident, a breakup with a boyfriend or girlfriend, a big fight with a friend, or a time of depression).

Totally New

The Topic: God's power

The Point: Students will learn that God is tremendously powerful! One example of that power is God's ability to completely change people's lives.

The Scripture: Acts 7:59–8:8; 9:1-20; Romans 1:16-17

The Object: Popcorn

The Supplies: You'll need Bibles; unpopped popcorn kernels; a popcorn machine or a kettle; ingredients for making popcorn (such as oil, butter, and salt); and symbols of power such as a battery, a barbell, money, a computer, and a diploma.

The Object Lesson

Before students arrive, set up a table in the middle of the room, and place the various symbols of power you selected on it.

When students arrive, prompt them to spend some time looking at the objects on the table.

Ask: • **How do each of those objects symbolize power?**

• **When have you seen or experienced an amazing display of power?**

Say: **Humans may gain power through strength, money, science, education, or politics—but human power is *nothing* compared to God's power! God's power is truly amazing.**

Have the students call out several examples of God's power using this statement to explain their ideas: "God has the power to…" Invite students to share examples of God's amazing power that they've experienced or learned about through the Bible.

Say: **One amazing example of God's power that we don't often think of is God's power to change lives. Let's take a look at one example of this power in the Bible.**

Have volunteers help you read Acts 7:59–8:8; 9:1-20 aloud.

Ask: • **What was Paul like before he met Jesus on the road to Damascus?**

• **How was he changed by God?**

• **How have you personally seen or experienced God's power to change lives? Explain.**

Give each student a single popcorn kernel, and ask students to describe the kernels—what they look like, what they smell like, their size and shape, and perhaps even what they taste like.

Say: **God has the power to *completely* change lives—not to partially change them or sort of change them or just modify them a bit—but to *totally* change them.**

Invite a volunteer to read aloud Paul's words in Romans 1:16-17.

Ask: • **How do these verses explain the changes that have taken place in Paul's life?**

• **How do these verses apply to your own life?**

• **How can these verses apply to the lives of non-Christian students at your school?**

Have students join you in a kitchen area and watch you pop popcorn in a kettle or a popcorn maker. Once the popcorn is popped, invite the students to each take a piece, look at it, and compare it to the unpopped kernel he or she has.

Ask: • **Describe all the ways this piece of popcorn is different from the original kernel.**

• **Can it ever go back to being the way it was before?**

Say: **God is not a wimp! He has the power to change lives completely—to give people hope, salvation, and righteousness! He can turn people away from empty and meaningless lives and provide them with purpose, joy, and direction.**

Have students form pairs and discuss how they want to experience God's power in their own lives or in the lives of specific non-Christian students they know. Invite them to pray together, holding their unpopped kernels while they pray as symbols of God's power to completely change people's lives.

When students have finished praying, invite them to eat some of the popcorn in celebration of God's awesome power.

Taking It Further

Study other significant examples of lives changed by God, such as the Samaritan woman at the well (John 4). Invite an adult member of your congregation to share a bit from his or her own life, specifically focusing on God's life-changing power in his or her life. Use this to prompt students to create short spiritual autobiographies, highlighting how they've seen God's power move in their own lives either by dramatically changing them or by gradually helping them to overcome particular habits or sins.

Cookie–Cutter Comparison

The Topic: God's will

The Point: Students will learn that they can all follow God even though they're different from each other.

The Scripture: 1 Thessalonians 5:14-18

The Object: Cookie cutters

The Supplies: You'll need Bibles, cookie dough, wax paper, flour, a rolling pin, cookie cutters, a spatula, cookie sheets, a blunt-edged knife, an oven, oven mitts, and napkins.

The Object Lesson

Have students gather around a table. On the table, place a batch of prepared cookie dough on a sheet of wax paper. Depending upon how sticky the dough is, you may need to sprinkle some flour on the wax paper first. Sprinkle some flour on a rolling pin, and begin rolling the dough to the thickness indicated by the recipe. Allow volunteers to help roll out the dough. As the cookie dough is being rolled out, discuss with students how they're all alike and how they're all different.

Ask: • **How are you similar to other people?**

• **What about you makes you unique?**

• **Do those qualities limit who you can be, what you can do, and how you can do things? Explain.**

FYI

You can make the cookie dough yourself ahead of time using a recipe of your choice; just be sure to use a dough that needs to be rolled rather than dropped in spoonfuls. If you'd rather not make your own cookie dough, you can find tubes of cookie dough in the refrigerated section of most grocery stores.

When you've rolled the dough to the appropriate thickness, explain that each person will have a chance to cut a cookie from the dough using a cookie cutter. Provide several different cookie cutters for students to use. Students can use any cookie cutter they like—they don't all have to be the same. Sprinkle some flour on the cookie cutters to keep them from sticking to the dough. After each person has pressed a cookie cutter into the dough, have him or her use a spatula to remove the cookie from the dough and place it on a cookie sheet. You may need to provide a blunt-edged knife to help separate the dough from the cookie cutter. Don't be concerned if a cookie is marred or broken; this actually will enhance the discussion.

After everyone has cut a cookie from the dough, gather students around the cookies.

Ask: • **How are these cookies similar and different?**

• **Are some of these cookies more "correct" than others?**

• **Is there one right way for all these cookies to be in order to be good cookies? Explain.**

• **What can these cookies demonstrate to us about different people who are trying to follow God's will?**

Place the cookie sheets into a preheated oven, and bake them for the time indicated in the recipe. While the cookies bake, have teenagers describe themselves, citing ways they think they're different from others.

Ask: • **Should everyone who is trying to follow God's will be the same? Why or why not?**

- **How do differences among God's followers bene-
  fit us?**

- **How do these differences lead to difficulties?**

Say: **Not everyone who is trying to obey God will be exactly the
same, as if they were all created with the same cookie cutter. As I look
around at all of you, I see people who are different from one another
but who are all trying to follow God's will. Let's see what the Bible
says about God's will.**

Ask a volunteer to read aloud 1 Thessalonians 5:14-18.

Ask: • **What does this tell us about God's will?**

- **What does this tell us about similarities and differences among people who are trying to follow
  God's will?**

Have students form groups of two or three. In their groups, have students discuss how they can follow God's will as described in 1 Thessalonians 5:14-18 in ways that reflect their different personalities. For example, if
someone is very musical, he could encourage others and share joy and
thankfulness through music. Or if someone is very quiet and shy, she could
share joy through one-on-one conversation and could thank God through
silent, reflective times. After a few minutes of discussion, ask volunteers to
share what their groups discussed.

Say: **The Bible tells us how to obey God. But there's not necessarily
one cookie-cutter way for us all to express our love for God and others. There are a lot of different options available. With our unique
variety of personalities, we can all be followers of God.**

When the cookies are ready, use oven mitts to remove the cookie sheets
from the oven. Allow the cookies to cool, and then serve them on napkins.

Taking It Further

Have students discuss the similarities and differences between following a cookie recipe and following God's will. Then have students form
groups and list other ways we can follow God—by loving God and our
neighbors, by following his commands, and by sharing our faith with others, for example. Provide concordances or Bible dictionaries for this segment of the lesson. Then ask each group to create a recipe for following
God's will. Groups should share their recipes with other groups. Finally,
have each teenager personalize a "recipe," citing how he or she can follow
God's will in a way that reflects his or her personality.

Take Time to Be Holy

The Topic: Holiness

The Point: Students will learn that God calls us to be holy.

The Scripture: Leviticus 20:7-8, 26; Colossians 1:21-22; 1 Peter 1:13-15

The Object: Aluminum foil

The Supplies: You'll need Bibles, aluminum foil, and markers.

The Object Lesson

Say: **Have you ever made an impression on someone? Has anyone ever made an impression on you? Today I'd like you to understand the impression God makes on each of us.**

Give each student a sheet of aluminum foil. Ask students to place the foil on their faces and form it to their faces. Give students a minute to do this, and then have students share their creations.

Aluminum foil has sharp edges. Remind students to be careful as they place the foil over their faces.

Say: **You've just made an impression of your face. The foil isn't you. It looks a little like you, but it's not you. It's a representation of what you look like. It's an impression of who you are.**

Distribute markers, and ask students to write their names on one side of the foil. Then have each student trade his or her foil with another student.

Faith Metaphors

Instruct students to shape the foil to their faces. When students have done this and admired their creations, have each person return the foil to its original owner.

Ask: • **What changed about your foil?**

• **What was the process you used to change the foil?**

Say: **Even though the foil has the name of the original person on it, it bears the resemblance of someone else. That's like holiness. We all look like ourselves, but we bear a resemblance to God.**

Have students form four groups (a group can be one person). Assign each group one of the following Scripture passages: Leviticus 20:7-8; Leviticus 20:26; Colossians 1:21-22; and 1 Peter 1:13-15. Ask groups to read their passages and decide what their passages say about holiness. Have each group share its findings with the entire class.

Ask: • **What effect does striving for holiness have on our lives?**

• **What's the difference between God's holiness and our attempts to be perfect?**

• **Why is it important to recognize God's holiness?**

Say: **Holiness is God's impression on us. While we still look physically like ourselves, God's call is to look like him in the ways we live and think. Spiritually we're called to be holy, just as God is holy. God wants us to follow him and be like him. He doesn't want us to conform ourselves to the standard that the world gives us—he wants us to conform ourselves to him.**

Have students take their foil pieces and use them to make representations of areas in their lives in which they want to reflect God's holiness. For example, a student might create a pair of lips to represent a desire to clean up his or her language. When they're ready, encourage students to get in groups of two or three and share their shapes. When they're finished, ask groups to close in prayer.

Taking It Further

To help students understand the Old Testament concept of holiness, lead them in a study of holiness. Try using the concept of the "Most Holy Place" (see Exodus 26:34) that God established when he gave directions on the building of the tabernacle.

Thirst No More

The Topic: The Holy Spirit

The Point: Students will learn that the Holy Spirit fills us with life, even during the toughest times!

The Scripture: John 7:37-39

The Object: Bottled water

The Supplies: You'll need a Bible and sealed plastic bottles of water (one for each student, plus at least four more).

The Object Lesson

Before the lesson, freeze four or more bottles of water. A few hours before the lesson, remove half of the bottles and allow them to partially thaw at room temperature.

Begin the lesson by giving each student an unfrozen bottle of water. Invite students to open their bottles and drink some water. (They can continue to drink their water throughout the lesson.)

Ask: • **What are some specific situations you've experienced in which you've really wanted or needed a drink of water?**

• **What does water do for us?**

Invite a student to read aloud John 7:37-39.

Ask: • **What type of thirst was Jesus describing? Explain.**

• **Jesus describes the Holy Spirit as a stream of living water that can satisfy our thirst. Based on what we just discussed, how is the Holy Spirit like water in our lives?**

• **How can the Holy Spirit satisfy our thirst?**

Invite the students to share personal examples of times the Holy Spirit has satisfied their spiritual thirst.

Faith Metaphors

Say: **Sometimes life can really feel like a desert. We can feel spiritually or emotionally drained. We can feel worn out and dried up. When we face trials, grief, frustration, loneliness, or disappointment, sometimes we don't exactly feel like we have a refreshing stream of living water flowing within us—sometimes we feel all dried up. Sometimes we feel spiritually frozen.**

Ask: • **Have you ever felt spiritually dried up or frozen? What made you feel that way?**

Pass around the unopened frozen bottles of water, and invite students to look closely at them as they are passed.

Ask: • **What do you notice about the frozen bottles of water?**

Say: **Sometimes we face really tough circumstances and situations in our lives. Like these bottles, we feel like we've been in a spiritual freezer. But even during those tough times, God's Spirit is still welling up inside of us like a fountain. God doesn't leave us during those times! In fact, his Holy Spirit, the Comforter, expands in us and fills the empty and lonely spots in our lives.**

Prompt students to observe how the water in the bottle expanded when it was frozen, changing the shape of the bottle and filling it to absolute capacity.

Ask: • **How has God's comforting Spirit filled you during tough times in your life? Explain.**

Ask two volunteers to stand in front of the others and give them the partially frozen bottles to open. When they unscrew the lids, some water will spill out of the tops of the bottles because of the pressure inside.

Say: **No matter how tough life can get, what Jesus said is always true. The Holy Spirit is like living water in our lives. Despite how we may feel during painful, difficult, "freezing" circumstances, God's Spirit can still flow within us, bringing life and comfort!**

Taking It Further

Take the water metaphor even further by using scientific facts about water to teach students more about the Holy Spirit. Not only is water a unique liquid because it expands when it freezes, but water also has several other interesting qualities, such as the way water repels other liquids such as oils. You can use these facts and others to teach about the way the Holy Spirit bonds Christians together or how the Holy Spirit enables us to resist sin. Invite one of your students who is a biology or chemistry whiz to help you put this lesson together.

The Straight Truth

The Topic: Honesty

The Point: Students will learn that because Jesus is truth, honesty is important for his followers.

The Scripture: John 1:14; 4:23-24; 14:6

The Object: Wire

The Supplies: You'll need Bibles and a six-inch piece of wire for each student.

The Object Lesson

Ask students to form groups of approximately four to six as you give each student a piece of wire. Ask students not to bend the wire yet.

Tell groups that each person will take a turn describing a lie or an occasion to lie that is common to high school students. For example, students might be tempted to lie when their parents ask if they got all their homework done or when their friends ask how they look. If students have told these kinds of lies, they should add a bend to their wire. Make sure each person gets at least one, if not two or three, opportunities to share. Students should continue to bend their wires for each kind of lie they've told.

> **FYI**
>
> Chenille wires will work if you have them, but you'll need to instruct students to make dramatic bends in them so that the "fuzzies" won't obscure the difference between the straight and bent wires. Craft wire is readily available at craft stores.

When groups have finished, say: **We sometimes talk about lies as "bending" the truth, as if bending it is really no big deal. But as you can see, there is a real difference between the straight wire I gave you and the wire you now hold.**

Ask students to spend a moment silently considering their wires and confessing to God their dishonesty.

Ask: • How do you feel about your wire? Explain.

• When do you find it easiest to lie? Why?

• Do you think others consider you to be an honest or dishonest person? Do you agree with their perception of you? Why or why not?

• Have you ever been caught in a lie? What happened?

• What are the advantages of living honestly? What are the disadvantages of dishonesty?

• Can there be advantages to dishonesty? If so, what?

Assign one-third of the groups to read John 1:14, one-third to read John 4:23-24, and one-third to read John 14:6.

Say: **The Gospel of John often talks about Jesus in terms of truth. After you've read your verse or verses, discuss these two questions:**

• What does this verse say about Jesus (or God)?

• What does this verse mean for us regarding truth?

After a few minutes, ask groups to read their verses aloud and share what they discussed.

Ask: • If Jesus is truth, what does it say about us as his followers when we lie?

• What do you think it means to worship God in truth? How can we do that?

• What practical ideas do you have for following Jesus more closely in honesty?

Say: **Jesus is full of truth—he is the truth—and we need to worship him in truth. That doesn't leave much room for dishonesty among his followers.**

Challenge students to keep their bent wires as reminders to follow Jesus in truth by being honest.

Taking It Further

Ask students to try to straighten their wires, and ask whether they can tell that the wire has been bent. Read 1 John 1:8-9, and lead a discussion on repentance and forgiveness. Ask questions such as "What does repentance mean to you?" and "How does it make you feel to know that God forgives all your sins?"

An Investment Worth Banking On

The Topic: Hope

The Point: Students will learn that hoping in God means investing in his promises—he will *not* disappoint us.

The Scripture: Psalm 62:5-7; Romans 5:5

The Object: A piggy bank

The Supplies: You'll need Bibles, a piggy bank, markers, and play money (one bill for each student).

The Object Lesson

Ask: • If I were to give you each one thousand dollars with only one requirement—that you invest it—what would you do with it? How would you invest it?

• What would be the absolute safest place to keep that money, with little or no risk of losing any of it?

Say: **When people put money in a bank, they have absolute confidence that their money will be safe. The bank is not going to call them one day and say, "Sorry, but we've gone broke, and all of your money is gone." We fully rely on banks to keep our money safe.**

Pass around the piggy bank.

Ask: • How is investing money in a bank similar to putting our hope in God?

• What does *hope* mean?

Have a student read aloud Psalm 62:5-7, and have another read aloud Romans 5:5.

Ask: • How do these verses describe hope?

• What do you think David, the writer of the psalm, meant by some of the word pictures he used here?

Say: **David said that God was the source of his hope. He trusted in God and his promises so fully that his honor and his reputation relied entirely upon God. He invested his whole heart in God. The Scriptures promise that hope in God will *not* disappoint us. Is *your* hope in God?**

Pass around play money and markers, and invite students to take a few moments to silently consider their own lives—have they invested their hope in God? Or are they relying on themselves or other things? Prompt students to think of specific areas of their lives in which they need to choose to put their hope in God instead of in their own abilities, another person, or any particular thing. Have the students each write down one word on the bill that summarizes the area or situation they thought of. Then pass the piggy bank around again and say: **Just as investors fully rely on a bank to take care of their money, putting our hope in God means we'll trust one hundred percent that he will not disappoint us. We know that he keeps his promises, and we rely on him completely.**

Give students an opportunity to demonstrate their hope in God by inviting them to fold their bills and put them in the piggy bank as it is passed around. Close by having all of the students look up Psalm 62:5-7 in their Bibles and read it aloud together.

Taking It Further

Consider expanding your discussion to include the many things people put their hope in that are disappointments in the end, such as good looks, money, financial investments, athletics, musical talents, or intelligence. Discuss the story of Job as an excellent example of what it means to fully invest one's hope in God alone and not in material or temporal things.

A New Perspective

The Topic: Justice

The Point: Students will learn that understanding God's heart for justice will change the way they view the world around them.

The Scripture: Isaiah 58:6-10; Amos 5:23-24

The Object: A magnifying glass

The Supplies: You'll need Bibles, several magnifying glasses, a book with small print, a detailed painting or picture, a map with small print, an ink pad, a piece of white paper, several pages from a newspaper, a magazine, and a *Where's Waldo?* book (optional).

The Object Lesson

Before students arrive, set out all of the supplies (except the magnifying glasses) on a table in the back of the room. Use the ink pad to put fingerprints on the sheet of white paper.

Begin by telling the students that they have just one minute to look at all of the items on the table. When the minute is up, have the students gather together, with their backs to the table.

Ask: • **Describe the objects on the table to me. What are some specific things you noticed?**

Ask the students other questions such as what geographic area was represented in the map, what the picture depicted, what the main headlines of the newspaper were, or what the title of the book was. Then say: **Now I'm going to give you another chance to examine the objects on the table in the back, but this time I'd like you to look at them through this.**

Hold up a magnifying glass and say: **Pay close attention to what you see, particularly what may be different from what you observed last time**.

Pass out several magnifying glasses, and ask the students to work together to use them to examine the objects on the table. Give them several minutes to do this, and encourage them to take their time examining details that they didn't notice before.

After several minutes, gather the students together again.

Ask: • **How was your perspective different when you looked through the lens of the magnifying glass?**

• **What details did you notice this time that you may not have noticed before?**

Prompt students to be very specific about their observations, such as describing details they noticed on the map that they didn't see before, describing the magnified appearance of the fingerprint, or describing the close-up appearance of the newspaper and magazine pictures.

Say: **In the same way we saw things with a whole new perspective when we looked through the magnifying glasses, we view the world through God's lens of justice and end up paying attention to important things that we may not have noticed before. Listen to these verses from the Old Testament that describe the way God's people** *thought* **they were pleasing God but were actually looking at worship with the wrong perspective.**

Have volunteers read Isaiah 58:6-10 and Amos 5:23-24 aloud.

Ask: • **Instead of worship music and fasting, what did God really desire of his people? Give specific examples.**

• **Why are these issues so important to God?**

• **How would you describe God's perspective on justice?**

• **How do these verses apply to us today? What are some unjust things in the world, in our community, and in our schools that we may not even notice or regularly overlook but that matter tremendously to God?**

• **How might your perspective of the world change if you viewed it through God's lens of justice?**

Challenge your students to look through the newspaper each day this week and to evaluate the events they read about using God's standard of justice. Close by praying together, asking God to give you a heart that loves justice the way he does and eyes to see and notice the problems in the world that greatly concern him.

Taking It Further

Use this opportunity to specifically address an area of social justice that is a problem in your community or local school, such as racism, poverty, unemployment, social ostracism, or bullying. Set up a specific project that you can work on with your students to address the issue, such as organizing a canned-food drive to feed the poor.

Familiar Words

The Topic: Knowing Jesus

The Point: Students will be challenged to study God's Word in order to obey it.

The Scripture: John 14:23

The Object: Speeches

The Supplies: You'll need a Bible and photocopies of famous sermons, speeches, and other documents. For example, use sermons by Jesus and Martin Luther King Jr. and speeches by John F. Kennedy and Abraham Lincoln. Use documents such as the Constitution and the Pledge of Allegiance. Well-known poems and lyrics to well-known songs can also be used.

The Object Lesson

Have students form groups of two to five. Say: **Today we are going to have a little test! I have copies of famous sermons, speeches and documents. Your job is to identify who delivered each speech or wrote each document, poem, or song.**

Give each group copies of the speeches, documents, quotes, and lyrics, and allow the students to get to work. Once the majority of the groups finish, go over the answers.

Ask: • **How did you know who gave the speeches or wrote the documents?**

• **Are you familiar with the people who gave these speeches or wrote these documents?**

- Can you tell me a little about each of these people based on what they said in their speeches or documents?

- Can you say that you know a person more once you have studied what he or she said?

Say: **Just as we may feel we know more about these writers and speakers based on what they wrote and said, we can get to know Jesus better by reading and studying what he said.**

Ask: • **How often do you read God's Word?**

- **How can you become really familiar with what Jesus says?**

- **Why do you think even pastors or Bible scholars still study Jesus' words even if they've already read them once?**

Say: **It's amazing that we have access to many of Jesus' actual words. Reading those words just once will not ensure that we know everything about Jesus. Every time we read the words of Jesus, we can get something new out of them.**

OK, let's go back to the documents.

Ask: • **Were you familiar with most of these documents? Explain.**

- **Is it important for you to follow what these documents say?**

- **Can you follow what they say if you don't read them?**

Have a student read aloud John 14:23.

Ask: • **What does this verse say about how we can love God?**

- **Do you try to learn about God's Word in order to obey it? Why or why not?**

- **What can you do if you don't understand God's Word?**

Say: **God gave us his Word! By reading about what Jesus said and did, we can know Jesus even more. We can love him by becoming familiar with his instructions and following them.**

Taking It Further

Have the students study parts of the Sermon on the Mount (Matthew 5–7) in small groups and share with the larger group what they learned about Jesus' character through their studies.

The Bodyguard Plus

The Topic: Leadership

The Point: Students will gain an appreciation for God's continual presence as they fulfill leadership obligations.

The Scripture: Joshua 1:9

The Object: A video clip of the president with a bodyguard and advisors

The Supplies: You'll need a Bible, self-stick name tags, markers, a video clip of the president with a bodyguard and advisors (either from the news or a scene from a movie such as *The American President, JFK,* or *Deep Impact*), a TV, and a VCR. Also provide various "bodyguard" accessories such as trench coats, toy guns, earphones, sunglasses, clipboards, and cell phones.

The Object Lesson

Write "President" on each of the self-stick name tags. You'll need one for each pair of students. Set out the bodyguard accessories on a table.

Ask: • Do any of you want to be leaders, such as the president, a king or queen, a military leader, or even the class president? Explain.

Have students form pairs, and give a "President" badge to each pair.

Ask: • How would it feel to be the president?

Say: **Let's watch a video of the president.**

Show the video clip.

Ask: • How do you think the president in this clip was feeling?

• Does it look like he does the job alone? Explain.

Say: **In your pairs, I'd like you to choose one person to be the president. That person will put on the name badge. The other person will serve as the president's bodyguard or advisor. I'd like this person to take one of these "accessories" to help him or her do the job.**

Ask: • Would you want to have bodyguards and advisors if you were the president? Explain.

• How do you think the president would feel if he didn't have bodyguards or advisors?

Say: **Most people in powerful positions don't do the job alone. They have advisors, spokespeople, and bodyguards. Let's read a Scripture about God's view of human leadership.**

Ask a volunteer to read Joshua 1:9 aloud.

Ask: • Why do you think God said this?

• Would Joshua have been a good leader without God's continual presence and help? Explain.

• Do you think that if you were in a leadership position you would do a good job without God's presence with you? Explain.

Say: **God doesn't always call the most confident, capable, "I-can-do-everything" type of person. He often calls people that will show his glory by relying fully on him to guard them, to protect them, and to advise them.**

Ask: • Why is it important for a person in leadership to rely fully on God?

Have pairs pray together that God can use them if he so desires in leadership roles in order to reveal his glory. Encourage pairs to pray for humility, wisdom, and discernment from God, both for themselves and for the present leaders of their school, church, city, and country.

Taking It Further

Have students look in concordances to find out about other leaders in the Bible like Moses, Gideon, and David. Discuss the biblical leaders' attitudes and how God used them. Encourage the students to examine their own attitudes when they are asked to fulfill leadership obligations.

Hearing Aids

The Topic: Listening

The Point: Students will learn to improve their friendships through the art of listening.

The Scripture: Proverbs 10:19; 18:13; 23:19

The Object: A "hearing" exam created from sounds and a song

The Supplies: You'll need Bibles, lined paper, and pens. You'll also need a blank cassette tape, an audiocassette recorder, and a recording of a song your students have never heard.

The Object Lesson

Create a taped "hearing" exam by recording ten different sounds onto a blank cassette tape. These should be common sounds, such as water running in the shower, a refrigerator door opening and closing, or someone walking up stairs. After these ten sounds, record on the same tape a song that your teenagers would never have heard.

Give each student a sheet of lined paper and a pen, and inform students they will be taking a pop quiz! Play the tape, and ask students to identify each of the sounds by writing their answers on their papers. When you've played all ten sounds, ask students to turn their papers over, lay their pens down, and listen to the recorded song. When the song is over, ask students to write down any words they can recall from the song they just heard.

Discuss students' answers and then say: **Sometimes it's surprising how much we miss—not just in the dozens of sounds that bombard us every day, but in important conversations with friends or parents or teachers. Think of all we could learn by improving our listening skills. Our grades might improve, we might know more about the people we care for, and we just might stop ourselves from saying things we'll later regret.**

Ask: • **What are some other benefits of being a good listener?**

Say: **The Bible emphasizes that wise people listen well, and it points out some of the consequences of being a poor listener.**

Ask volunteers to read Proverbs 10:19; 18:13; and 23:19 aloud.

Ask: • **How can listening make you smarter and more discerning?**

• **How can listening make you a better friend?**

• **How can talking too much get you into trouble?**

• **How can you win friends just by being a good listener?**

Discuss different ways to exercise listening skills. You might suggest things like keeping a small pocket notebook nearby to write down needs or prayer requests friends might share, taking notes at church and at school, learning as much as possible about someone you don't know very well, and thinking about the lyrics to the songs you listen to.

Use the pattern in the margin to create a giant ear out of cardboard. Add some color and simple details with markers. Cut a hole in the middle of the ear to form the ear canal. On the back side of the hole, use duct tape to attach an empty plastic grocery bag. Place the different verses from Proverbs on slips of paper, and put them inside the bag. Have students reach into the ear and pull out the verses one at a time. Throw some cotton swabs into the bag for added fun. Some additional verses to include are Proverbs 12:18; 13:3; 17:27-28; 20:12; 21:13; 23; 22:17-18; 23:22; 24:32; and 29:20.

Taking It Further

If time allows, have students form pairs. Encourage partners to take turns learning about each other. You might want to provide questions to prompt the discussion, such as "What is your family like?" and "What are your hobbies?" After partners have had an opportunity to practice their listening skills, ask them to share the details they learned about their partners with the rest of the class. This will not only exercise students' listening abilities, it will also help them get to know each other better.

Out of the Square

The Topic: Love

The Point: Students will learn that love sees beyond social categories.

The Scripture: Luke 19:1-10

The Object: A chessboard and chess pieces

The Supplies: You'll need Bibles, a chess board, and chess pieces.

The Object Lesson

Set out a chess board, and place the different chess pieces on one side of the board. Gather students around the board, and ask them to name each piece. Have teenagers discuss the different characteristics they'd give each chess piece—what characteristics fit a queen, a knight, and so on.

Then ask students to discuss where on the board the different chess pieces belong. Have volunteers help you set up the board for play.

> **FYI**
>
> If you don't have chess players in your group, have students help you place the chess pieces on different squares. Instead of emphasizing the correct positions of chess pieces on the board, simply emphasize that each chess piece is to fit into its own square.

Ask: • **How does this chess board reflect the way our society functions?**

• **How does our society label people?**

• **How does our society determine where people belong because of the role they play?**

Have students form pairs and talk to each other about how they themselves have been treated as "chess pieces." Encourage students to discuss how society has labeled them and told them where they do and do not belong.

Ask: • **How does it feel to be labeled?**

• **How does it feel to be told where you do and do not belong?**

• **How do you think others feel when you label them and assume that they do or do not belong?**

Have youth look up Luke 19:1-10 in their Bibles, and then ask a volunteer to read the passage aloud.

Ask: • **In what different ways was Zacchaeus labeled?**

• **Where was his place in society? How do you know?**

• **How does Jesus' love for people affect how he sees others?**

• **How can our love for people affect how we see them?**

• **If we saw others the way Jesus saw Zacchaeus, what do you think would change?**

Gather the group around the chess board again. Ask each person to hold a chess piece, look carefully at it, and name one thing about the piece that he or she didn't notice before. Then give everyone a chance to remove a chess piece from the board.

Say: **It's easy to see people according to labels. It's pretty natural for us to categorize things. But when we treat people or limit them according to labels, we're putting them into too-tight squares. When we do that, we're not loving others—or ourselves—as Jesus does.**

Taking It Further

Provide a stack of magazines for students to look through. Encourage students to cut out pictures of people and use markers to label them as society labels them.

Ask: • **Where does each labeled person belong on the chess board of society? Why?**

• **If we loved these labeled people the way God loves us, how would we see them differently?**

Have youth place sticky notes or masking tape over each written label and then write on the tape a better way to see that person.

Hot Stuff

The Topic: Making a difference

The Point: Students will learn that they can make a difference in the lives of others.

The Scripture: Matthew 5:14-16

The Object: Hot sauce (the hotter the better)

The Supplies: You'll need Bible, tortilla chips, hot sauce, a pitcher of ice water, cups, plates, and napkins.

The Object Lesson

FYI

It's best to have bread or milk on hand to "neutralize" the effects of the hot sauce. Water is good but not as effective. It is also a good tip to recommend to students that they keep the hot sauce from touching their lips to minimize the "heat" they'll experience. If you have time, you may also want to allow students to tell stories of the hottest sauces they ever ate, just for fun.

Give each student a plate, and pass around the tortilla chips, encouraging each student to take a handful. Have students eat a few of the chips. Tell them to remember the taste of the chips. Then show students the hot sauce. Challenge them to place even just a drop of the sauce on their chips. Encourage as many students as possible to try the hot sauce.

Ask:
- **Describe the taste of the chips without sauce. How did they taste with sauce?**
- **It didn't take much hot sauce to make a difference in the taste of these chips. What are some other things that are small but make a big difference?**
- **Would you say you make a difference in the lives of others? Explain.**

Say: **You have been created for God and his good pleasure. He has made you to make a difference in this world and in the lives of others. Let's learn more about that.**

Read Matthew 5:14-16 aloud.

Ask: • **What does Jesus mean when he calls his disciples "the light of the world" and a "city on a hill"?**

• **How can we let our light shine before others?**

• **What are some things we can do that could cause others to praise our Father in heaven?**

• **What "small" thing has someone done for you lately that made a big difference to you?**

• **What small things have you done lately that made an impact on someone else or "touched" them in some way?**

Say: **Each one of us was made to make a difference on this earth for God and in the lives of others—sometimes it's the small things we do that make the biggest differences. God has gifted each one of us with talents, abilities, and aspects of our personalities that are absolutely unique. He's given us these things to accomplish a specific purpose. For some of us, these gifts are obvious. Others may have to try a little harder to find their gifts, but they are there for us to find and share. But the biggest gift God has given all of us is the gift of love. Because of God's love for us, we can all love without limits.**

Have students form small groups of three or four, and encourage each person to share how he or she can love others or use his or her gifts, talents, and personality to make a difference in the lives of others.

Taking It Further

Create cards with chili peppers drawn on the fronts with the words "You're Hot Stuff to God" written on them (make one for each student). Write each student's name on a card, and display the cards on one wall of the room. Then have students rotate around to the different cards, writing on them any of the following: a gift, talent, or positive characteristic of the person named; a good deed or act of kindness they observed the person doing; or some unique quality or characteristic the person brings to the youth group or class. Move around the room and make sure all cards are written on and that what is being written is positive and affirming. Read 1 Thessalonians 5:11 aloud and close in prayer.

Promises, Promises

The Topic: Media

The Point: Students will learn that they can rely on God's promises.

The Scripture: Genesis 17:15-16; 21:1-2; Exodus 3:16-17; 12:40-41; Numbers 23:19; Joshua 23:15-16; 1 Chronicles 17:11-14; 2 Chronicles 36:15-19; Matthew 3:16-17

The Object: Recorded and printed media

The Supplies: You'll need Bibles, a stereo, an audiotape recording of songs, magazines, newspapers, a TV, a VCR, a videotape recording of commercials, music videos, movies, and popular TV shows.

The Object Lesson

FYI

If you don't have time to record television or radio, simply have groups flip through TV channels or scan through radio stations, pausing to watch or listen to a couple of minutes of different programs and commercials. You can also use any media you have at hand. If a computer with an Internet connection is available, supervise students as they look at different Internet sites. You can even look at billboards if there are some near your meeting area.

Have students form three groups. Have one group gather around the stereo, have the second group gather around the TV, and have the third group gather around a pile of magazines and newspapers. Challenge youth to critically review the media and define the promises they make. Have the TV group play the videotape, have the stereo group play the audiotape, and have the printed-media group look through the magazines and newspapers. Remind students to evaluate not just the advertisements, but also the program material or articles. For example, a TV show may be promising that selfishness leads to financial success, a news article may be promising that people who commit horrible crimes become famous, and a song may be promising that violence against women solves relationship issues.

As groups evaluate the media, have them discuss the following questions:

Ask: • **Why do you think the song, article, or show makes this promise?**

- **Do you have faith that this promise is true and will be fulfilled? Why or why not?**

After each group has had at least five minutes to survey the media, have everyone gather together. Ask each group's members to share what they learned about the promises the media make.

Ask: • **What other kinds of promises do the media make?**

- **Of the many promises the media make, how many do you think they can fulfill for you personally?**

- **How much faith do you put in promises people make? Why?**

- **What do we learn from the media about promises?**

Say: **The media use promises to sell to us. Companies who produce media understand that we'll pay attention—which of course results in more money for them—if they promise to change our lives for the better. Unfortunately, most media promises don't stand the test of time.**

Now let's look at some other promises.

Distribute Bibles, and have volunteers look up and read aloud the following pairs of Scriptures:

- Genesis 17:15-16; 21:1-2
- Exodus 3:16-17; 12:40-41
- Joshua 23:15-16; 2 Chronicles 36:15-19
- 1 Chronicles 17:11-14; Matthew 3:16-17

After volunteers read the Scriptures, have the group discuss them.

Ask: • **What promises did these Scriptures contain?**

- **How have the promises been fulfilled?**

- **How are biblical promises different from and similar to advertising promises?**

Ask students to find Numbers 23:19 in their Bibles and read the verse aloud together.

Ask: • **What does this Scripture say about the difference between God's promises and promises made by the world?**

- **Do you have faith that God's promises will be fulfilled?**

Say: **The world's promises are often manipulative and fleeting. But the world doesn't set the standard for trustworthiness. God does. God has never broken a promise. God's record throughout the Bible stands as testimony that God is faithful. Faith is believing that God will fulfill what God has promised.**

Taking It Further

Have students form groups of four or five. Ask each group to create a commercial that honestly conveys what a product can provide; groups can talk about products they saw advertised in the TV commercials they watched. Then have each group create a commercial that honestly conveys what God can provide. Afterward, have groups discuss the difference between what the media can provide and what God can provide.

This Little Light

The Topic: Money

The Point: Students will learn that they have a responsibility to use their money and other gifts wisely.

The Scripture: Matthew 25:14-30

The Object: Taper candles

The Supplies: You'll need Bibles, taper candles, and matches.

The Object Lesson

You'll need to do this object lesson in a room that can be made completely dark.

Begin by asking:

- **What's your attitude about money? Are you a wise investor, a "put-it-under-the-mattress" type, or a "shop-'til-you-drop" type?**
- **How do you think God feels about money?**

Have students form three groups.

Say: **We're going to use these candles and a Bible passage to help us understand how God feels about money.**

FYI

You may want to have a flashlight handy to help the groups see well enough to light the candles.

Have a volunteer read Matthew 24:14-18 aloud. Say: **Instead of talents of money, I'm going to give you candles.**

Give the first group one candle, the second group four candles, and the third group ten candles. Say: **Now let's see what this might have looked like.** Provide each group matches, then turn out the lights.

FYI

To avoid wax "drip-page," cut holes in index cards and put them about halfway up the candles. This will catch the wax and keep it from dripping on students' hands or on the floor.

Have the first group light its candle.

Ask: • **How much light does this little candle give off?**

Have the people in the group form a tight circle around the person holding the candle to hide its light.

Ask: • **Now how much light can you see?**

Say: **You've buried this light, much as the man in the story buried his one talent of money.** Have the first group blow out its candle.

Have the second group light two of its candles. Say: **The second man invested his talents of money and made twice as much.** Have the group use the first two candles to light the second two candles.

Ask: • **Now how much light can you see?**

Say: **You've multiplied this light, much as the man in the story invested wisely and made his money grow.** Have the second group blow out its candles.

Have the third group light five of its candles. Say: **The third man also invested his talents of money and made twice as much.** Have the group use the first five candles to light the second five candles.

Ask: • **Now how much light can you see?**

Say: **You've multiplied this light, much as the man in the story invested wisely and made his money grow.** Have the third group blow out its candles, and turn the light back on.

Say: **Now let's hear the rest of the story.** Have a volunteer read Matthew 25:19-20 aloud.

Ask: • **What did the master want his servants to do with the money he gave them?**

• **Who does the master represent? the servants?**

• **What does this Scripture tell you about God's views toward money?**

Say: **Everything that we have, including our money, is a gift from God. We have a responsibility to use our money and our other gifts wisely. When we share our money and use it wisely, it can grow and become much more for God.**

Taking It Further

Create a series of lessons on stewardship. As an ongoing project, give each student a certain amount of money and challenge them to "grow" their money in a certain amount of time. At the end of the time, have students bring the money they gained and share their stories. Use the money for a mission project.

Obedience, the Loving Choice

The Topic: Obedience

The Point: Students will learn that God has designed us to obey him, not as mindless robots but as loving children.

The Scripture: John 14:21

The Object: A remote control

The Supplies: You'll need Bibles, a remote control, and the appliance that goes with the remote control.

The Object Lesson

Begin the object lesson by showing various things you can do with the remote and appliance. As you speak, stress how much control you have

over the appliance because of the remote. Then have students take turns with the remote using it to "control" the group. Students should each be given the remote to hold for thirty seconds. During that thirty seconds, they can give the group any command they like and the group must obey just as an appliance would.

Ask:
- **How is this remote-control power over the appliance like or unlike God's control over us? Explain.**

- **Why do you think God didn't just create us without free will—why didn't he make us like robots who always do as he commands?**

- **What does this tell you about God and his view of us? his love toward us? Explain.**

Read John 14:21 aloud.

Say: **In this passage, Jesus links obedience to God with love for God, and he gives us some pretty cool promises.**

Ask:
- **What three things does Jesus promise to those who have his commands and obey them?**

- **Why do you think Jesus promises to show himself to us when we love him through our obedience to him?**

- **Why do you think God puts such a value on our choice to obey him and his commands?**

- **Why do you think he responds to our loving obedience with an outpouring of love of his own?**

Have students form pairs and share with their partners one way they most need to obey God. (For example, someone might say he or she needs to treat someone kindly that has been mistreated in the past.) Partners should encourage one another and offer advice about how to obey God in the areas they shared. After they have encouraged one another, ask partners to pray for each other.

Taking It Further

As a group, create a banner mural with the heading "What God Loves!" or "Ways to Make God Smile." Draw or list on the banner all the actions and attitudes that would please God by showing loving obedience to him and his commands.

Then have students form teams and work in these teams to list on poster board or a dry-erase board areas in which they believe it is most difficult to obey God. Then have students discuss each of these difficult areas and think of different actions and attitudes that will help them obey God in these areas the next time they experience difficulty.

Family Resemblance

The Topic: Parents

The Point: Students will learn that for better or worse, they resemble their parents.

The Scripture: 2 Timothy 1:5

The Object: A mirror

The Supplies: You'll need a Bible and one hand-held mirror for every group of five.

The Object Lesson

Have students form small groups of up to five. Give each group a mirror.

Say: **I've got some good news and some bad news. Let's start with the *good* news: You resemble your parents.**

Now here's the *bad* news: You resemble your parents.

It starts with the DNA. Even kids who grow up apart from their biological parents bear some resemblance physically and medically. And when you're raised in a family, you assimilate the values and attitudes of your parents—like it or not.

In your groups, starting with the person whose birthday is closest to today, I'd like you to look in the mirror and then pass it to the right. While you're looking in the mirror, share one thing you see that reminds you of your parents and that you wish you could change about yourself. The members of your group can ask you up to five questions about what you say.

Give groups time to complete this exercise.

Say: **Now send your mirror back around your circle. This time look in the mirror and share one thing you see that reminds you of your parents that you *don't* want to change—ever.**

When groups have finished, ask a volunteer to read aloud 2 Timothy 1:5.

Ask: • **Could Paul write these words about your family? Why or why not?**

• **What's an interest, hobby, or talent you think you've inherited from your family?**

Say: **Paul doesn't mean Timothy inherited his faith in God. It doesn't work that way. But Timothy certainly benefited from being raised in a household of godly women who pointed his heart and mind toward God.**

In their small groups, have teenagers discuss the following questions:

Ask: • **In what ways did your parents contribute to your being here and being open to growing in your Christian faith?**

• **Parents have plenty of faults. That's a given. But what's something you see in one or both of your parents that you admire?**

Say: **When we were very young, we looked at our parents and thought they were wonderful. Then, as we grew older, we realized they're just like everyone else: human. They have faults. They sometimes disappoint us and themselves. News flash: They're not perfect.**

But they *are* our parents, and in one way or another we'll resemble them as long as we live.

We have another parent, too: God. He *is* a perfect Father, and as we grow in our love for him and grow in our faith, we begin to resemble him. We reflect his values and attitudes because we begin living in a way that pleases God. Let's pass the mirror around one more time. This time, look into your eyes as you hold the mirror and share one way you believe you're coming to resemble your heavenly Father.

Invite teenagers to pray for each other in their groups.

Taking It Further

Invite students to write down their parents' admirable qualities and then share the notes with their parents as affirmations. Explore further what it means to be a Christian son or daughter (Colossians 3:20-21).

Real Peace

The Topic: Peace

The Point: Students will learn that real peace comes when we look at life from Christ's perspective.

The Scripture: Psalm 46:1-3

The Object: Crushed seashells

The Supplies: You'll need a Bible, a small bucket, and crushed seashells.

The Object Lesson

Fill the bucket with the crushed seashells.

Ask: • **What things make you feel afraid?**

• **How do your body and mind respond when you feel afraid?**

• **What things make you feel at peace?**

• **How does your body and mind respond when you experience these things?**

Say: **Life is full of events and issues that make us fearful. From scary movies to painful issues like divorce and death, life is full of things to be afraid of. We've already talked about what happens to your body when you feel afraid. Your palms start to sweat (not to mention your armpits!), your heart starts to race, and your breathing gets shallow. Even though you try hard to look like you're not afraid, your body and mind react strongly to things that cause you to feel afraid. But God wants to bring you true peace, even when you face things that scare you.**

Have a volunteer read Psalm 46:1-3.

Ask: • Imagine what David was feeling when he wrote this psalm. What do you think he was afraid of?

• David showed his reliance on God in this psalm. Why do you think people sometimes find it difficult to rely fully on God when they are afraid?

Show students the broken seashells in the bucket.

Say: **The key to really understanding God's peace is in this little bucket.**

Ask: • What do you see in this bucket?

Say: **These shells represent perspective. When we look at life through our own human lenses, we often only see things that make us afraid. But when we try to see things from God's perspective, we may see them differently. This can help us to gain real peace.**

Dump the bucket of shell pieces on a table. Invite each student to choose several pieces. Encourage students to find the most beautiful pieces of shell they can find. As they find their pieces, share the following story:

A woman and her son traveled to the beach together every summer. Each year they would collect shells along the water's edge. One summer they collected sand dollars. The next year they collected snail shells. They always tried to find the most perfect, beautiful shells.

One summer was a bit different. The boy looked inside the pail his mother was holding.

"Why are you collecting broken things, Mom?" he asked.

His mother just smiled, picked up a broken shell, and examined it closely.

"What do you want that one for?" the boy questioned. "It's not perfect."

"That's why I want it," his mother responded. "Just because it's not perfect. It's broken, but it's still beautiful. Kind of like the relationship your dad and I have right now. We are working through some things that are not perfect. I know that makes you feel afraid."

"Yes, it does," the boy said, perplexed.

"Well," his mother responded gently, "I'm not afraid if it's not perfect. I'm satisfied with the beauty I can find in the broken piece."

The boy picked up a handful of broken shells off the sandy ground. "So that must be some kind of secret to life. Finding the beauty in something you can't always see as beautiful."

"And, that my son," she said, rubbing his back, "brings peace. Real peace. Seeing the beauty in what seems to be broken."

Ask: • The broken shells represent areas of our lives that make us feel afraid. What are some broken pieces in your life?

Say: **God has a way of bringing peace in our lives when we see things from his perspective. The broken shells represent the broken pieces in our lives that can cause us to be afraid of life's outcomes before anything even happens. Even things that make us afraid can become beautiful when we look at them through God's lenses and not our own. When we can truly see the beauty in things, we can begin to understand God's peace, no matter what our circumstances are.**

Taking It Further

Have an open, honest discussion about some of the things in life that cause us to feel afraid. You may want to explore things such as divorce, separation, failure, problems at school, difficult friendships, and sickness. Take each area and look at it through God's perspective, citing biblical examples in which God gave people incredible peace despite what they were facing.

A Way Out

The Topic: Peer pressure

The Point: Students will be encouraged to know that they can stand up to peer pressure and temptations.

The Scripture: 1 Corinthians 10:13

The Object: A window frame

The Supplies: You'll need Bibles and a window frame.

The Object Lesson

Have students sit in a circle.

Ask: • **Have you ever faced peer pressure? Explain.**

• **What exactly is peer pressure?**

Say: **Peer pressure often means that other people pressure us to do things. These things can be either good things or bad things.**

Ask: • **What kinds of things do peers sometimes pressure others to do?**

• **What do you think God's view of peer pressure is?**

• **How can God help you deal with peer pressure in your life?**

Pass the window frame around the circle and have each student look through it.

Ask: • **Have you ever heard the expression "If you can't use the door, look for the window"? What do you think it means?**

• **When we're tempted to give in to peer pressure, how do you think God can help?**

• **Do you think God provides a window out of temptation? What might this window look like?**

Read 1 Corinthians 10:13 aloud.

Ask: • Do you think God lets us be tempted beyond what we can bear?

• According to this verse, do we have an excuse for giving in to peer pressure? Explain.

• Do any of you have a story about being pressured and taking the way out God gave you?

Say: **Let's go back to the things that peers sometimes pressure others to do.**

Choose a few of the pressures, and discuss each one with students, encouraging them to think of things that God provides them with so that they won't fall into sin.

Taking It Further

Break the students up into small groups, and have them create skits about common pressures they all might face and ways out using the windows God provides them with. Each group can actually use the window frame in its skit. Encourage the students to be creative as they think of their "windows" out.

Prayer Perfume

The Topic: Prayer

The Point: Students will learn that time spent with God in prayer has a lasting effect on the entire day.

The Scripture: Psalm 61:1-4

The Object: Perfume

The Supplies: You'll need a Bible, a bottle of perfume, facial tissues, and several blindfolds.

The Object Lesson

Spray a small amount of perfume onto facial tissues, and give a tissue to each student.

Say: **Take a deep sniff of the tissue I have given you.**

Ask: • **How does the scent on the tissue make you feel?**

• **How long do you think the fragrance will last?**

• **Are there certain perfumes that remind you of someone or some event?**

Have students give the tissues back to you, and divide the group into teams of four or five. Give each team a blindfold, and have members of each team choose the person with the best "sniffer." Say: **We are going to try a little exercise to demonstrate the power of the nose. Blindfold your team's sniffer.**

Give each team one of the perfumed tissues. Have them hide their tissues somewhere in the room. Say: **Let's see which sniffer can find a tissue first. As your sniffer sniffs out the tissue, you can't speak to him or her or lead him or her toward the tissue. Your job is to stand close by and gently guide your sniffer away from any hazards.**

After several teams have found their tissues, bring the group back together.

Ask: • **Why was it difficult to find the tissue?**

• **How did remembering the scent help you find it again?**

• **How could this be similar to remembering times we have spent with God in prayer?**

Say: **When we pray, the fragrance of being in God's presence stays with us for a long time, just like the scent on the tissue. And when we find ourselves in difficult situations, we can cling to the conversation we had with God earlier.**

Read aloud Psalm 61:1-4. Say: **God promises that he, like perfume, will never leave us or forsake us. Prayer is our way of spraying his lasting scent on us.**

Taking It Further

Encourage students to scatter throughout your meeting area or even outside. Give them several minutes to spend in prayer, worshipping God and spending time in his presence.

Free at Last!

The Topic: Salvation

The Point: Students will learn that when they experience Christ's salvation, they are set free from sin and eternal destruction and are given abundant, eternal life.

The Scripture: John 8:36; Romans 5:18-19; 6:1-7

The Object: Handcuffs

The Supplies: You'll need Bibles, a stopwatch or a watch with a second hand, and a set of handcuffs with a key for every two students. If you can't find enough pairs of handcuffs, use twine and scissors to create them.

The Object Lesson

Have students form pairs, and give each pair a set of handcuffs. Have partners handcuff themselves together, and have each partner choose one of two "identities"—the good identity or the bad identity. Tell students that you'll time them for one minute. During that minute, those who chose the bad identity will say or do wrong things, such as make faces, say rude things, or try to steal other people's things. Those who chose the good identity will say or do good and kind things, such as giving compliments, offering help to others, and smiling. Each partner should try to encourage others to act as he or she is acting. Make sure everyone understands and then start the clock. When time is up, keep everyone handcuffed and lead a short discussion.

Ask: • **Describe your experience of being handcuffed to someone with an opposite mission to yours.**

Say: **Listen to this Bible passage about the sin of Adam and the righteousness of Christ.**

FYI

As close to the beginning of the lesson as possible, be sure to offer a brief explanation of salvation according to the teachings of your church, since there will likely be students present who do not know what salvation is. We experience salvation when we accept Christ and believe that he died on the cross for our sins, that he was buried, and that he rose again three days later so that we can go to heaven when we die and live abundant and satisfied lives in relationship with him.

Read aloud Romans 5:18-19; 6:1-7; and John 8:36.

Ask: • **Explain what the "trespass" (disobedience) was that caused all people to be condemned.**

• **How did Christ's obedience bring us grace, righteousness, and eternal life?**

• **How was the person we were handcuffed to that did what was wrong like our "old self" or body of sin (as described in Romans 5)? How was the person we were handcuffed to that did what was right like our new self, living a "new life"? Explain.**

• **How is being handcuffed to someone who only wants to do wrong like your life before salvation?**

Set students free from their handcuffs.

Ask: • **How is being set free from sin through Christ like being freed from these handcuffs—and free from our old selves?**

Have students share with the group some things they feel Christ's salvation has changed in their lives or set them free from. Then have them mention things Christ has set them free to do, like loving others with an unlimited love, or new promptings he has given them, such as a strong desire to do what is right. Close by praying for all the students to not just break away from the habits of their old selves, but to break *toward* doing all the right and good things of their new selves in Christ.

Taking It Further

Have students work together to list on dry-erase board or poster board all the things that Christ's salvation sets them free from—such as sin, destruction, and hell. And have them list all the things Christ's salvation sets them free to do—to love others with an unlimited love, to be unselfish, to be like Christ with lives that bear all the fruit of the Spirit.

Read aloud 2 Corinthians 5:17-21. Discuss what it means to be a new creation in Christ. Talk about what the message of reconciliation is, what our ministry of reconciliation is all about, and what it means to be Christ's ambassadors. Finally discuss practical ways to communicate with friends and loved ones Christ's promise of becoming a "new creation" and being given "new life." Challenge students to come up with ways to communicate what it means for Christ to set us free and the new life that "freedom in Christ" brings.

The Pearl of Purity

The Topic: Sexual purity

The Point: Students will learn that sexual purity is a special gift from God.

The Scripture: 1 Corinthians 6:19-20

The Object: An oyster shell

The Supplies: You'll need Bibles, a plastic "pearl" for each student, and two oyster shells—one closed oyster shell and one open oyster shell with a pearl sitting inside it. (Oyster shells can be picked up at a local grocery store seafood department. Ask for a sealed oyster shell and one that has opened. You may need to keep the sealed oyster in water. Make sure the shell is sealed by trying to pry it apart. If you can't open it, your students will most likely not be able to either.)

The Object Lesson

Ask: • **What messages do you get from our society about sex before marriage?**

Encourage students to brainstorm popular television shows, movies, or songs that depict the acceptance of sex before marriage.

Say: **Did you know that the mind is considered the strongest sex organ of all? It activates all sexual hormones in the body. The mind can be trained to say yes and no regarding different things that stimulate it.**

Ask: • **What's something in your life that you said yes to even though you should've said no?**

Say: **Sexual purity is one of the toughest issues most of us will face during our young adult years. But if we can grasp self-control when we're young, we'll build a foundation that lasts our entire lifetime.**

Hold up the sealed oyster shell. Say: **Let's see if any of you can open this sealed oyster shell.** Encourage students to pass around the shell and try to open it. It won't be easy! Most oyster shells are extremely difficult to crack.

Say: **Unless you forcefully open the shell with your hands or use an object to crush it, you won't be able to open an oyster shell. Most oysters** hold on to the pearls inside pretty tightly. An oyster won't open up its shell until the pearl is finished. The oyster closes its shell so tightly so that it will not give away prematurely what is most treasured.

Have a volunteer read 1 Corinthians 6:19-20 aloud.

Ask: • **How does Paul say we should treat our bodies in this passage?**

• **How does this oyster symbolize our purity?**

• **Why do you think the world gives away what is most treasured so easily?**

Say: **Our sexuality is just like the oyster that holds a pearl. It's a gift that must not be opened until the right time. If it's given away too early, the treasure is stolen before it's ready.**

Ask: • **How do you think a person feels when he or she has given his or her sexual purity away?**

Say: **Someone who gives his or her sexual purity away prematurely may try to hide behind a mask of fulfillment, but that person may feel guilty, awkward, and regretful. Why? Because God created us to save the sacred treasure of our virginity until we're married. When we prematurely give it away, we're left with a lot of feelings to sort through.**

Hold up the open oyster with the pearl in it. At the same time, hold up the closed oyster you have passed around the group.

Say: **God wants us to save the treasure of purity so that when he's ready for us to enjoy the great gift of sexuality in marriage, the gift is a beautiful pearl that is pure and sacred. If we allow ourselves to be pried, poked at, and crushed, we'll miss the beauty God created for us to enjoy in marriage.**

You may ask what a person can do if he or she has already been sexually active and given his or her treasure away. An oyster uses sand and dirt to create a pearl. The oyster takes those dirty, impure elements and turns them into a beautiful pearl. In the same way, God can take the impurities in your life and turn them into something of great beauty and value. If the sacred treasure of your sexual purity has been given away already, hold tightly to the dignity you have through the cross of Christ. Close yourself from this painful choice, and allow God to take all the wrong choices and turn them into a beautiful pearl again. Although the consequences of our choices remain, **God has an awesome way of taking the dirt in our lives and turning it into treasure if we trust and follow him.**

Give each student a pearl. Ask your students to make a pledge to live lives of pearl-like purity. Encourage several volunteers to pray for the group, and be ready to pray in private with any individuals that may need special prayer regarding this sensitive issue.

Taking It Further

Set up an accountability structure between leaders and students. It's best to pair same-sex leaders and students. Have accountability groups or pairs meet periodically to share together areas in which they have been vulnerable or have failed. Encourage prayer, Scripture memorization, and relationships that glorify God rather than wrongly fulfill emotional or sexual needs.

Is There a Doctor in the House?

The Topic: Sharing faith

The Point: Students will learn that it's important to share their faith.

The Scripture: Colossians 4:2-6

The Object: A jar filled with small candies

The Supplies: You'll need Bibles, a jar filled with small candies, scrap paper, pencils, and a basket (or bowl).

The Object Lesson

Say: **Before we get started, I have a rather unusual request. I want you to think of the disease that scares you most. Don't be funny about it—I want an honest answer. Think of the one disease that you would absolutely hate to have. Write your answer on a piece of scrap paper.**

Distribute scrap paper and pencils, and give students a moment to write. Then ask students to fold their papers and put them aside until later.

Say: **OK, now we can get on with this activity! Today we're going to be discussing sharing our faith.**

Have students form pairs to answer the following questions. After each question, invite partners to share their answers with the rest of the class.

Ask: • **When is a time you shared your faith with someone? What happened?**

• **When is it hard for you to share your faith? Why?**

• **Have you ever wanted to share your faith, but you didn't do it? Describe that situation.**

Give each person another piece of scrap paper.

Say: **We all have times when it's difficult to share our faith. I want each of you to write one excuse you might give for not sharing your faith. For example, you might write, "I would feel stupid," "I'd be laughed at," or "I don't know what to say."**

Give students time to write, then have them place their papers in the basket. Bring out the jar with the candies in it, and hold the jar up for everyone to see.

Say: **Let's say that I have in this jar the wonder drug of all time. This medicine can cure even the most hopeless disease! Let's also say I'm the** *only* **person in this town who has this medicine.** Have students retrieve the papers on which they wrote the diseases they fear most. **And finally, let's say that you're dying of the disease you wrote on your paper, and I have the cure.**

Tuck the jar of candies under one arm, and have students stand next to each other in a line. Go up to each student individually. Have each student say, "I'm dying of (the disease he or she wrote). Can you help me?" Answer each student by saying, "I *could*, but…" Then read an excuse from the basket. After you've gone all the way through the line, ask the following questions. After each question, invite volunteers to share their answers with the rest of the class.

Ask : • **If these candy pills really were miracle drugs and you really were sick, what would have happened if I had given them to you?**

• **How is a miracle pill or cure like knowing about Jesus?**

• **How can knowing about Jesus save your life?**

- **How did you feel when I gave an excuse instead of giving you the medicine you needed in this activity?**

- **How is that like not sharing your faith in Jesus with someone who needs to hear about him?**

Say: **We're all dying of the disease called sin. And Jesus is the only cure. Without Jesus; we have no chance of eternal life. I know a Bible passage that says it better than I can.**

Have students read Colossians 4:2-6.

Ask: • **What does this passage say to you?**

  • **How can these verses help you share your faith?**

Say: **If someone we knew were dying of a disease, and we had the cure, we wouldn't hesitate to give it. Why should sharing our faith be any different? What's a little embarrassment or discomfort compared with someone's eternal salvation? People *need* the cure of Jesus—they'll die without it.**

Pass around the jar of candies, and let each person take one. As they take a candy, have each student say the name of one person they can tell about Jesus. Then close in prayer, asking God to give your students the strength and courage to share their faith.

Taking It Further

During this activity, have students take each excuse they thought of for not sharing their faith and come up with a solution. Then have students role-play situations in which it's difficult for them to share their faith. Having them practice in a nonthreatening place can help them carry through the next time they're debating whether to share the good news of Jesus.

Faith Metaphors

Short Circuit

The Topic: Sin

The Point: Students will learn that sin separates us from God and disrupts our relationships with him.

The Scripture: Isaiah 59:1-2, 20

The Object: Christmas lights

The Supplies: You'll need Bibles, a string of Christmas lights, several replacement bulbs, two large pieces of poster board, and a marker.

The Object Lesson

Before the lesson, check your string of Christmas lights to make sure that the entire string (as well as your replacement bulbs) works. Locate at least one bulb in the string that, when removed, will cause all or some of the remaining lights on the string to go off. Use a marker to color the tip of that bulb.

Begin by asking students to name some really "big" sins, and write them on one of the poster board pieces.

Then ask the students to name "smaller" or more common sins, and create a new list on the second poster board piece. Prompt students to think of some sins they commit every day, perhaps without even noticing, like pride, gossip, or selfishness.

Point to the "big sins" poster.

> **Ask:** • **What effects can these sins have on a person's relationship with God?**
>
> • **How about the "small" sins we listed? Do you think they affect our relationship with God? Explain.**

Plug in your string of Christmas lights (you can attach several strings together if you'd like), and have one student pick up the end and stretch it across the room. Invite all of the students to sit on the floor along the string of lights and hold a portion of the string in their hands.

> **Ask:** • **How is our relationship with God like the flow of electricity in this string of lights?**

- **What are some of the things you love most about your relationship with God?**

Have one student read Isaiah 59:1-2 aloud. Then remove the marked bulb from the string of lights. (This should cause all or part of the string to go dark.)

Ask: • **What does this passage tell us about God's character?**

• **According to this passage, what can sin do to our relationship with God?**

• **Have you ever experienced what this passage describes? Explain.**

Say: **The Scriptures say that our sin creates a separation between us and God—it short-circuits our relationship. It doesn't matter if it's a "big" sin like the ones we mentioned earlier or if it's something that seems "small." All of our sins hinder the awesome relationship God wants with us.**

Invite each student to think of one specific sin that has recently (or is currently) hindering their relationship with God. Once a student has thought of something, have him or her carefully remove a light bulb from the string as an illustration of the short circuit the sin has caused.

Ask: • **What can you do to make your relationship with God right again when you've sinned?**

Read aloud Isaiah 59:20 and ask: • **What does it mean to repent?**

Say: **The good news is that God did send his Son, Jesus, as our redeemer, just as this Scripture prophesies. Through faith in him, we can find salvation and forgiveness for our sins. Yet even when we've placed our faith in Jesus, sin can still creep in and hurt our relationship with him. However, God's grace and forgiveness are available for any sin we commit, no matter how great or how small. Choosing to practice repentance can restore that broken relationship.**

Have the students take a few moments to silently pray, and prompt them to privately confess any sins, big or small, that they feel may be hindering their relationship with God. Then invite them to replace their light bulbs into the string as a symbol of the complete restoration that results from true repentance. As students are replacing their light bulbs, replace the one you removed earlier as well. The entire string of lights will then be illuminated again.

Say: **We are *all* sinners—we'll never be perfect and we'll never stop messing up. But we don't need to walk around moping and feeling terrible for every small sin we commit. The great news is that God** *never* stops loving and never stops forgiving! So, instead of letting sin short-circuit your relationship with God, make it a practice to regularly examine your heart, confess your sins to God, and accept his full forgiveness. Instead of letting sin dim the lights, keep your relationship with God shining brightly!

Taking It Further

Study David's sin of adultery with Bathsheba and his repentance in 2 Samuel 11–12 and Psalm 51 with your students. Use Psalm 51 as an example of true repentance, and encourage students to use it as a model to create their own prayers of confession.

I Am the Church...

The Topic: Spiritual gifts

The Point: Students will learn that everyone has an essential part in building the church.

The Scripture: 1 Corinthians 12:12-27

The Object: Building blocks

The Supplies: You'll need Bibles, children's building blocks, a watch with a second hand or a stopwatch, and crayons.

The Object Lesson

Gather enough children's building blocks so each student will have one block. You'll need to have assorted colors of blocks. Hide each block in a different place in the meeting room.

When students arrive, have them sit wherever they want in the meeting room. Say: **Today we're going to construct a tower. I'll need your help—each of you will need to bring your own block to help build the tower, and it won't be complete until each of you brings a block. I've hidden one block for each of you in this room, and I'm giving you thirty seconds to find them.**

Give students the signal to begin looking, and call time in thirty seconds.

If any students haven't found blocks, have the rest of the class quickly help them find some. Have students gather in a circle in the center of the meeting room. Say: **You've got complete freedom to build the tower however you'd like. I'd like the entire group to decide the shape, height, and general construction of the tower.**

Encourage group members to work together to complete the tower. When they're finished, have students form trios.

Ask: • **How are these blocks like the church?**

• **What spiritual gifts might these blocks represent?**

• **What spiritual gifts are necessary for building the church?**

Say: **Each of you had an important part in this exercise. Without your block, the tower wouldn't have been built in the exact way you just built it.**

Ask trios to read 1 Corinthians 12:12-27 and discuss the following questions in their groups.

Ask: • **Why is the body of Christ important?**

• **Why are different gifts important?**

• **What would happen if everyone had the same gift?**

When groups are finished with the questions, ask volunteers to share what their groups talked about. When everyone has responded, ask students to each take a block from the tower and find a place in the room where they can be alone.

Ask: • **What's your place in the body of Christ?**

Allow students time to think about the question. After a minute, give each student a crayon. Ask students to write on their blocks one way they contribute to the body of Christ. When they're finished, have students form pairs and share what they wrote.

FYI

If you're using blocks that can't be written on, consider placing a piece of masking tape on each block and ask students to write on the tape.

Say: **God has given each one of you a unique gift. He's called you to use your gift to help build the body of Christ. You are an essential block in God's plan. God is counting on you to use the gifts he gave you to build his church.**

Have students gather together and rebuild the tower. When they're finished, ask students to look at the tower. Ask each student to share aloud what he or she wrote on the block and how that gift can help build the body of Christ. When students are finished sharing, have them pray and ask God to help them be bold as they use their gifts to build Christ's church.

Taking It Further

To help students understand their places in the body of Christ, invite someone from your church to give them a spiritual gifts test. Make sure that you ask your volunteers to lead several sessions to help students understand their gifts and how their gifts can be properly used in the church.

No Pain, No Gain

The Topic: Spiritual growth

The Point: Students will learn that they won't grow spiritually unless they exercise their faith.

The Scripture: James 2:14-17

The Object: Tennis ball

The Supplies: You'll need Bibles and one tennis ball for each student.

The Object Lesson

Have everyone gather around you. Hold up a tennis ball in each hand for all to see.

Ask: • **What are these?**

• **What are they used for?**

• **What are some other uses for these tennis balls?**

Say: **Tennis balls are obviously used for playing tennis. But these balls can also be used for conditioning and building strong muscles. When we exercise our muscles, they grow stronger and healthier. I'll show you what I mean.**

Hold a tennis ball in each hand. Slowly squeeze one tennis ball as you bend your elbow and raise your forearm, as if you were lifting a dumbbell.

Lower that arm and repeat the process with the other arm. Alternate arms, performing several repetitions for each arm, making sure students see that you're squeezing the tennis balls tightly. Then stop and ask students the following questions:

Ask: • **Wow, that's great exercise—don't you feel stronger?**

• **Did you feel your heart rate go up as I exercised?**

• **Couldn't you just feel your arms getting stronger as I squeezed the tennis balls?**

Have students form pairs, and give each pair two tennis balls. Let partners decide who will exercise first. Have the first partner in each pair hold both tennis balls and squeeze the balls in sequence, just as you did in your demonstration. Walk around the room and encourage the partners who aren't exercising. Feel their biceps and make comments such as, "Wow, these exercises are really working!" and "Good job, keep it up!" Encourage the exercising students to make similar comments to their partners. Call time, have partners switch roles, and repeat the process.

Collect the tennis balls, and have students answer the following questions with their partners. After each question, have partners share their answers with the rest of the class.

Ask: • **What was wrong with this activity?**

• **Why didn't watching your partner squeeze the tennis balls help your arms grow stronger?**

• **Why can't watching someone else exercise build strong muscles for you?**

• **What do you have to do to build strong muscles?**

Say: **This activity really did have a point to make. Turn in your Bible to James 2:14-17, and read the verses with your partner.**

Pause as students read. Then ask a volunteer to read the verses aloud.

Ask: • **What do you think these verses mean?**

• **Do you see any connection between spiritual growth and growing strong muscles? Explain.**

Say: **Just as we can't grow strong muscles without exercising, we can't grow spiritually without exercising our faith. Watching someone else exercise doesn't build our muscles. And having faith but not** using it doesn't help us grow spiritually. True faith requires action, or that faith is dead.

Ask: • What excuses do people sometimes give for not exercising?

• How are those excuses similar to why people don't exercise their faith?

Say: **The similarities between physical exercise and spiritual exercise are interesting. People** *intend* **to exercise. They're** *inspired* **when they see others get in shape. They** *get ready* **to exercise—they buy the equipment and the supplements. But often, they just never find the time or motivation to carry through. It's just too hard.**

Ask: • What's hard about exercising?

• What makes people want to quit an exercise program?

Say: **When we exercise, we may feel temporary pain. We get short of breath, and our muscles hurt. Sometimes we want to quit. Even though we know our bodies will grow stronger if we continue, it may seem too hard.**

Sadly, it's often the same way with spiritual growth. People want to grow in their faith. They listen to inspirational speakers, and they buy books and tapes. But when an opportunity for spiritual exercise arises, they often back away.

Ask: • When do you think you're more likely to grow spiritually—during easy times or hard times? Why?

• When is a time you've grown spiritually?

Say: **We often grow the most spiritually when we're faced with problems and tough times. Just as hard exercise produces strong muscles, hard circumstances can produce strong faith. The next time you're faced with a problem, don't back down. Think of the tennis ball exercise. Persevere. Don't give up. Most of all, turn to God. Trust him to work in the situation, and you'll find your faith growing as a result.**

Taking It Further

Have students identify the problems and situations that present stumbling blocks to their spiritual growth. Do they struggle with peer pressure? Sharing their faith? Bad habits they just can't shake? Let students write their answers in personal journals to refer to later. Or let students create their own barbells with balloons and cardboard tubes, and have them write their answers on the balloons.

Then have partners look up Scripture verses that can help them in those situations. Make sure students write the Scripture references in their journals or on their barbells. Then have partners pray for each other, asking God to help their faith grow strong.

Pushed to the Popping Point

The Topic: Stress

The Point: Students will learn that they can reduce the stress in their lives by opening themselves up to God's design for their lives.

The Scripture: Philippians 4:4-7

The Object: Dry ice

The Supplies: You'll need Bibles, masking tape, small pieces of dry ice, latex or rubber gloves, plastic film canisters, measuring tape, and screwdrivers.

The Object Lesson

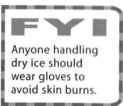

FYI
Be sure the teenagers don't point the film canisters at each other.

FYI
Anyone handling dry ice should wear gloves to avoid skin burns.

Use masking tape to create a starting line at one end of the meeting area. Divide the teenagers into teams, and give each team a film canister. Wearing gloves, place a small amount of dry ice in the bottom of each canister. Have each team place the lid on its canister, stand behind the starting line, aim the canister at the other end of the room, and wait. As the canister caps begin to blow off, measure the distance from the starting line to each lid's landing point to determine which team blew its top the furthest.

Ask: • **What made the lids blow off the film canisters?**

Faith Metaphors

- Why did some shoot farther than others?

- How is this like the way stress affects our lives?

Say: **Let's do a little experiment. I'd like you to poke a hole in your lid.** Give each team a screwdriver to use to poke a hole. Place another piece of dry ice in each team's canister. Have teams put the lids back on the canisters and wait to see if the lids still blow off.

Ask: • **What effect did a small hole have on the end result?**

• **How might this be similar to letting God into our lives?**

Say: **When we become stressed by people and decisions in our lives and we do not allow God to be part of those relationships and decisions, our stress increases until we finally explode. But when we begin to place our burdens and stress into God's hands, the pressure escapes and keeps us from exploding.**

Read aloud Philippians 4:4-7.

Ask: • **How can the strategy discussed in this passage help us deal with stress?**

• **What does the phrase "and the peace of God, which transcends all understanding" mean?**

Say: **Think about the biggest area of stress in your life.**

Ask: • **If you allow God to put a hole in that stress and relieve some of the pressure, what will the result be?**

Close in prayer, encouraging students to commit their stress to God.

Taking It Further

Spend some time in extended silent prayer and quiet time with God. Encourage students to use the time to release their stresses into God's care and spend time resting in his peace.

Magnetic Desire

The Topic: Temptation

The Point: Students will learn that God gives them the strength to resist the things that tempt them.

The Scripture: Hebrews 2:14-18

The Object: A magnet

The Supplies: You'll need Bibles, different sizes of nails, and several different sizes of magnets.

The Object Lesson

Divide the group into smaller groups based on the number of magnets you have available (you'll need one magnet for each group). Distribute a small handful of nails to each group. Make sure each group has nails of several different sizes.

Ask: • **Why are nails drawn to a magnet?**

• **Why are some nails drawn faster to the magnet than others?**

Say: **Let's do a little experiment. I'd like each group to decide which nail you think will be drawn fastest to the magnet. Do not test them yet; just guess.** Give members of each group time to decide which nail they think will be drawn fastest to the magnet. Then have each group place the nails in a circle with the points about two inches from the center. Have each group choose a person to stand above the nail circle and begin to slowly lower the magnet toward the center of the circle until one of the nails jumps up and sticks to the magnet.

Ask: • Were you surprised by the nail that was most easily pulled toward the magnet? Why?

• How could you have stopped the nail from being drawn toward the force?

Say: **Just as a nail is pulled toward the force of a strong magnet, so are we drawn toward the force of temptation. God does not tell us that there will be no things to tempt us when we trust him, but he does say he will help us resist temptation's powerful force.**

Ask: • What are some of the things that tempt us, that draw us in?

Read aloud Hebrews 2:14-18.

Ask: • Who is this passage talking about?

• How does Christ's experience on earth help us deal with temptation?

Say: **Let's try another experiment.** Have each group join with another group. Say: **Choose one of your "weakest" nails. Position the nail you've chosen on the ground between your two groups. Now begin to move your group's magnet toward the nail until one of the two magnets pulls the nail to it.**

Have the groups try this experiment.

Ask: • Why did one magnet "win" over the other?

• How is this like God in our lives?

Say **God desires to be the strongest force in our lives. If we allow him to draw us in and hold us close, just as the magnet did to the nail, we will not be drawn toward the things that tempt us.**

Taking It Further

Have students talk about various temptations they face in their lives. Then work as a group to come up with strategies for avoiding and overcoming those specific temptations with God's help.

Wise Up

The Topic: Wisdom

The Point: Students will learn that wisdom is a whole lot more than brain power—we demonstrate wisdom by how we live our lives.

The Scripture: 1 Corinthians 1:17-21, 27-31

The Object: No. 2 pencils

The Supplies: You'll need Bibles; paper; sharpened No. 2 pencils; a sample of the SAT or the ACT (available from high school guidance counselors or SAT/ACT prep books); a stopwatch or a watch with a second hand, permanent markers; a video recording of a TV quiz show such as "Jeopardy!" "Who Wants to Be a Millionaire," or "Weakest Link" (optional); and a TV and VCR (optional).

The Object Lesson

Before the lesson, select six extremely difficult questions from the test sample and create copies of your short six-question multiple choice quiz for your students. If you'd like, you can play the clips from television quiz shows throughout the lesson with the sound muted.

When students arrive, give each person a sharpened No. 2 pencil.

Ask: • **What does a No. 2 pencil make you think of?**

Say: **No. 2 pencils are special in one very important way—they're used to fill in the bubbles on standardized tests. Colleges and universities use standardized tests to determine if someone is "smart" enough to attend their schools. How many of you have had to take a standardized test, like the ACT, the PSAT, or the SAT?**

Ask: • **What was the experience like?**

Hand out copies of the six-question quiz and say: **Now you're going to have another chance to "test" your smarts. These six questions are real sample questions from an actual SAT** (or ACT) **test.**

Give the students only two minutes to complete the quiz by selecting the multiple-choice answers that they think are right. When the time is up, ask students to stop writing, and then reveal the correct answers to the test.

Ask: • So how was it? Did you get all the answers right?

Invite students to share their feelings about the questions, particularly if the quiz experience made them feel dumb or confused.

Ask: • Do you think those six test questions were truly able to test your intelligence? Why or why not?

• How does the world measure intelligence and wisdom?

• In your opinion, how does that compare to God's perspective on wisdom?

Say: **In several places in God's Word, we read about wisdom. Let's take a look at a passage that compares human wisdom with God's kind of wisdom.**

Read aloud 1 Corinthians 1:17-21, 27-31. Invite the students to follow along in their own Bibles.

Ask: • This passage compares two different perspectives on the message of the gospel. According to this Scripture, how does the world view Jesus' life, death, and resurrection?

• What have you heard or experienced in life that reflects this same attitude toward Jesus and Christianity?

• According to verses 30-31, where can we find true wisdom? How is this different from human standards of wisdom and intelligence?

• Which do *you* aspire to more—what the world considers to be wise and intelligent, or what God considers to be truly wise? Explain.

• What are some examples of ways we can live out God's wisdom in our daily lives? Be specific.

• How are the choices we make in life similar to using a pencil to mark bubbles on an exam?

Ask all of your students to hold their pencils in front of them. Say: **Throughout the next few years of your life, you'll have to use No. 2 pencils to fill in the bubbles on a whole lot more tests. And each time you sit down for an exam, you'll use your pencil to make important** choices—to fill in the bubbles that represent what you believe are the right answers.

Consider for a moment that your pencil represents your life, and just like filling in the bubbles on a test, you're choosing what you value every day. You choose what is really important to you—you choose what you believe is right.

Ask: • Have you ever had to choose between trying to impress others or focusing on embracing God's wisdom, even when others may have thought you were foolish? Explain.

• If someone were to create an exam (like the short one we took earlier) that measured God's kind of wisdom in a person's life, what types of questions would be on it?

• How can the choices you make demonstrate your wisdom (or lack of wisdom)?

Close by inviting students to read 1 Corinthians 1:17-21, 27-31 again in their Bibles. Ask students to each select one verse from the passage that stands out to them. Have students use markers to write the verse references on their pencils, and then prompt them to take the pencils to school and use them during classes for taking notes and exams as a reminder of the type of wisdom that God truly values.

Taking It Further

Dig deeper with your students into the Bible's book of wisdom—the book of Proverbs. Select several proverbs that emphasize the same principles as 1 Corinthians 1:17-21, 27-31. Then invite students to write their own proverbs using modern examples and current language. You also may want to provide the students with background information about Solomon's life. Point them to Scriptures about when he lived out true heavenly wisdom. Then contrast those Scriptures with ones that show how he made unwise choices and exhibited earthly wisdom (toward the end of his life.)

Topical Index

Scripture Index

Group Publishing, Inc.
Attention: Product Development
P.O. Box 481
Loveland, CO 80539
Fax: (970) 679-4370

Evaluation for
Faith Metaphors

Please help Group Publishing, Inc. continue to provide innovative and useful resources for ministry. Please take a moment to fill out this evaluation and mail or fax it to us. Thanks!

• • •

1. As a whole, this book has been (circle one)

not very helpful   very helpful

1   2   3   4   5   6   7   8   9   10

2. The best things about this book:

3. Ways this book could be improved:

4. Things I will change because of this book:

5. Other books I'd like to see Group publish in the future:

6. Would you be interested in field-testing future Group products and giving us your feedback? If so, please fill in the information below:

Name_____

Church Name _____

Denomination _____ Church Size _____

Church Address _____

City _____ State _____ ZIP _____

Church Phone _____

E-mail _____

Exciting Resources for Your Youth Ministry

At Risk: Bringing Hope to Hurting Teenagers

Dr. Scott Larson

Discover how to meet the needs of hurting teenagers with these practical suggestions, honest answers, and tools to help you evaluate your existing programs. Plus, you'll get real-life insights about what it takes to include kids others have left behind. If you believe the Gospel is for everyone, this book is for you! Includes a special introduction by Duffy Robbins and a foreword by Dean Borgman.

ISBN 0-7644-2091-7

All-Star Games From All-Star Youth Leaders

The ultimate game book—from the biggest names in youth ministry! All-time no-fail favorites from Wayne Rice, Les Christie, Rich Mullins, Tiger McLuen, Darrell Pearson, Dave Stone, Bart Campolo, Steve Fitzhugh, and 21 others! You get all the games you'll need for any situation. Plus, you get practical advice about how to design your own games and tricks for turning a *good* game into a *great* game!

ISBN 0-7644-2020-8

The Youth Worker's Encyclopedia of Bible-Teaching Ideas

Here are the most comprehensive idea books available for youth workers. With more than 365 creative ideas in each of these 400-page encyclopedias, there's at least one idea for every book of the Bible. You'll find ideas for retreats and overnighters...learning games...adventures...projects...affirmations... parties... prayers... music...devotions...skits...and more!

Old Testament	ISBN 1-55945-184-X
New Testament	ISBN 1-55945-183-1

Awesome Worship Services for Youth

These 12 complete worship services involve kids in 4 key elements of worship: celebration, reflection, symbolic action, and declaration of God's Truth. Flexible and dynamic services each last about an hour and will bring your group closer to God.

ISBN 0-7644-2057-7

Discover our full line of children's, youth, and adult ministry resources at your local Christian bookstore, or write: Group Publishing, P.O. Box 485, Loveland, CO 80539. www.grouppublishing.com

More Resources for Your Youth Ministry

New Directions for Youth Ministry

Wayne Rice, Chap Clark and others

Discover ministry strategies and models that are working in *real* churches...with *real* kids. Readers get practical help evaluating what will work in their ministries and a candid look at the pros and cons of implementing each strategy.

ISBN 0-7644-2103-4

Hilarious Skits for Youth Ministry

Chris Chapman

Easy-to-act and fun-to-watch, these 8 youth group skits are guaranteed to get your kids laughing—and listening. These skits help your kids discover spiritual truths! They last from 5 to 15 minutes, so there's a skit to fit into any program!

ISBN 0-7644-2033-X

Character Counts!: 40 Youth Ministry Devotions From Extraordinary Christians

Karl Leuthauser

Inspire your kids, introduce them to authentic heroes, and help them celebrate their heritage of faith with these 40 youth ministry devotions from the lives of extraordinary Christians. These brief, interactive devotions provide powerful testimonies from faithful Christians like Corrie ten Boom, Mother Teresa, Dietrich Bonhoeffer, and Harriet Tubman. Men and women who lived their faith without compromise, demonstrated Christlike character, and whose true stories inspire teenagers to do the same!

ISBN 0-7644-2075-5

On-the-Edge Games for Youth Ministry

Karl Rohnke

Author Karl Rohnke is a recognized, established game guru, and he's packed this book with quality, cooperative, communication-building, brain-stretching, crowdbreaking, flexible, can't-wait-to-try-them games youth leaders love. Readers can tie in these games to Bible-learning opportunities or just play them.

ISBN 0-7644-2058-5